Cambridge Elements

Elements in the Philosophy of Martin Heidegger
edited by
Filippo Casati
Lehigh University
Daniel O. Dahlstrom
Boston University

HEIDEGGER ON ETHICS

Mahon O'Brien
University of Sussex

CAMBRIDGE
UNIVERSITY PRESS

Shaftesbury Road, Cambridge CB2 8EA, United Kingdom

One Liberty Plaza, 20th Floor, New York, NY 10006, USA

477 Williamstown Road, Port Melbourne, VIC 3207, Australia

314–321, 3rd Floor, Plot 3, Splendor Forum, Jasola District Centre,
New Delhi – 110025, India

103 Penang Road, #05–06/07, Visioncrest Commercial, Singapore 238467

Cambridge University Press is part of Cambridge University Press & Assessment,
a department of the University of Cambridge.

We share the University's mission to contribute to society through the pursuit of
education, learning and research at the highest international levels of excellence.

www.cambridge.org
Information on this title: www.cambridge.org/9781009460002

DOI: 10.1017/9781009460019

First published 2025

A catalogue record for this publication is available from the British Library

ISBN 978-1-009-46000-2 Hardback
ISBN 978-1-009-46004-0 Paperback
ISSN 2976-5668 (online)
ISSN 2976-565X (print)

Cambridge University Press & Assessment has no responsibility for the persistence
or accuracy of URLs for external or third-party internet websites referred to in this
publication and does not guarantee that any content on such websites is, or will
remain, accurate or appropriate.

Heidegger on Ethics

Elements in the Philosophy of Martin Heidegger

DOI: 10.1017/9781009460019
First published online: March 2025

Mahon O'Brien
University of Sussex

Author for correspondence: Mahon O'Brien, mahon.o-brien@sussex.ac.uk

Abstract: Heidegger is often understood to have forsaken the very possibility of ethics – we find numerous variations of this view in the secondary literature. And yet, in *Letter on Humanism*, Heidegger stresses the importance of ethics (thought anew as originary ethics) in the context of the dangers posed by the technological age. In this Element, the author will try to unpack what Heidegger might have meant by this. Ultimately, his account of the essence of the human being will prove to be the key to understanding what he describes as 'originary ethics'.

Keywords: Heidegger, Ethics, Humanism, Metaphysics, Ontology

ISBNs: 9781009460002 (HB), 9781009460040 (PB), 9781009460019 (OC)
ISSNs: 2976-5668 (online), 2976-565X (print)

Contents

Introduction

> *Power objected . . . that he was tired of nationality and wanted to be international, like all the great writers. 'They were national first,' Joyce contended, 'and it was the intensity of their own nationalism which made them international in the end . . . I always write about Dublin, because if I can get to the heart of Dublin I can get to the heart of all the cities of the world.* ***In the particular is contained the universal****.*
> (Ellmann, 1982: 505. Emphasis Added)

I have had several false dawns with this Element. Finding 'a way in' proved challenging, and, for a period of time, I couldn't see clearly where or how I should begin. After all, Heidegger had effectively dismissed ethics as a viable philosophical enterprise, had he not? This appeared to be a prevailing view in the literature, even among those commentators who argued that one could think through some ethical ideas with Heidegger (often 'with' Heidegger but 'against' Heidegger), despite the latter's apparent foreclosure of that domain of questioning. How then could I contribute anything worthwhile? Why write a short Element on Heidegger and ethics if the upshot is that one will be submitting views that are not effectively Heidegger's or a book that is, for the most part, negative, that is, explaining why Heidegger dismisses the very idea of ethics?

There was then, of course, not just the proverbial elephant in the room but a herd of elephants stampeding around the house any time I tried to get some part of the enterprise off the ground. The stampeding registered as a series of loud remonstrations: 'Heidegger was a card-carrying member of the Nazi party!' 'Heidegger was the first Nazi Rector of Freiburg University in 1933!' 'Heidegger's vocal support for Hitler and his foreign policy in the early 1930s was nothing short of repugnant!' 'Heidegger was an antisemite – his private notebooks from the 1930s are teeming with incriminating and definitive evidence!' All of this is true. The file 'against' Heidegger on these issues continues to swell: his remarks on the historylessness and worldlessness of the Jewish people, 'Semitic nomads', what have you; his use of terms like *Verjudung* (Jewification) as he decries, for example, the 'Jewification' of German Universities; his despicable attempt to destroy the career prospects of Eduard Baumgarten, owing (among other things) to Baumgarten's association with 'the Jew Frankel' (but ultimately due to a petty grievance that attests to the vindictiveness of a man possessed of quite an extraordinary capacity for jealousy) – we could chronicle the offences over many, many pages and it would make for damning testimony indeed. There was the further matter of the character of the man. He has been portrayed as a mendacious philanderer and an arrogant, ruthless careerist with very few redeeming qualities.[1] Why on Earth would we

---

[1] See O'Brien (2015, 2020, 2022).

enlist the work of such a person to discuss ethics? I hope, in the pages that follow, the answer will become clear.[2]

My 'way in', then, as is so often the way with philosophical progress, was a sort of epiphany. I don't mean to suggest a religious experience in any conventional sense, but something closer to the Socratic idea of *anamnesis*, a seeing again of what one already knew but in a new way – a recognition that somehow seems new and familiar at the same time. Years ago, while finishing my doctoral thesis on Heidegger, I had a similar experience during the course of some routine morning tasks at my childhood home in a valley in the West of Ireland. What felt like a minor breakthrough all those years ago involved some sudden clarity concerning time, nothingness, and being in Heidegger. My thrownness and sense of being historically grounded in this particular place – the sounds and scents that drifted up the valley and that seemed to somehow form an invisible chain reaching back to my childhood – opened the door to some of Heidegger's fundamental ideas. It was the gift of my placed thrownness that once again played a pivotal role for this project, as I struggled to come to terms with Heidegger's comments concerning the urgent need to rethink ethics given the threats posed to humanity in the technological age. It also allowed me to get clear on the correctives needed to forestall the problematic ways that Heidegger attempted to mobilise his own thinking in the 1930s.[3] In such a short text, I cannot pretend to have offered something comprehensive or exhaustive. However, I hope at least to have indicated a 'way in' to the question of the relevance of Heidegger's thinking for ethics.[4]

1 The 'Way' In

The greatest care must be fostered upon the ethical bond at a time when technological man [humanity], delivered over to mass society, can be kept reliably on call only by gathering and ordering all his [its] plans and activities in a way that corresponds to technology. (GA9: 353/268)

When hiking through the countryside, according to a well-known anecdote, Heidegger was known to stop at chapels and wayside shrines, dip his finger in the stoup (before making the sign of the cross presumably), and genuflect.

---

[2] That is not in any way to suggest that I am disavowing my robust criticisms of Heidegger in some of my other work, where I take him to task for his illegitimate attempts to mobilise aspects of his own thought in the service of a despicable political vision.

[3] I elected not to engage directly with these issues in this Element. I have directed readers to my own engagement with these issues as and when they are relevant to the discussion at hand.

[4] I would like to thank Paul Davies, Christos Hadjioannou, Alex Obrigewitsch, Conor Edwards, and Michael Jonik for comments and feedback on earlier drafts. I would also like to thank Cambridge University Press's anonymous reviewer for their generous and constructive feedback.

Often, when I recall this story, I am prompted to reflect on my own childhood. I grew up in a rural, Catholic community in the 1980s in the West of Ireland where such acts would have been commonplace, undertaken as much out of habit as anything else. I am still inclined to quickly make the sign of the cross in certain situations; if I am attending a religious ceremony for a friend or relative in a Catholic church, I normally dip my fingers in the stoup and make the sign quickly upon entering and leaving. It happens almost as a reflex; often I'm already in the midst of the activity or have finished before I begin to wonder as to its legitimacy or significance. After all, I don't actually *mean* to invoke the Christian God; whatever meaning it is imbued with is as much historical and cultural for me as anything else. And yet, it is certainly not an empty gesture.

Sometimes, upon realising what I've done automatically, I begin to think of how the Catholic church was very much a focal point of the local community and how such habits and customs were a part of my daily life. A stream of associated memories often follows: a noisy phalanx of schoolchildren rushing along the footpath to mass in St Peter's Church, Broadford, Co. Clare each morning of Lent – before we run back along the main street, through the village to the school after mass, just in time for roll call. I sometimes recall the nervous anticipation of my first morning as an altar boy, the distinctive odour of the vestry – a musky, aromatic mixture of candle wax, wood polish, and faded incense; clouds of incense smoke belching from the thurible and images of somnolent mourners shuffling behind a coffin out of the church to the appointed slot in the graveyard outside – the pit covered for now but with the tell-tale, horrifying mound of freshly dug Earth heaped beside it; my exhilaration when it was my turn in the rotation to carry the paten during Holy Communion; rapidly intoned Hail Marys and Our Fathers – interweaving lines chanted in lockstep of increasing cadence building to mini crescendos at the wake of a neighbour or relative; images of the Stations of the Cross that fascinated and horrified me as a I sat in a cold pew, in silent turmoil at the depictions of the most gruesome torture on the walls, yet unable somehow to resist fixating on the tormented cruciform figure in the final scenes.

As I walk down a busy street in Brighton, in the south east of England (where I have been living now for some time), surrounded by the colour and spectacle one might associate with a summer afternoon in this part of the world, the glimpse of a hearse slipping by can pull me out of the lively, carnival-like atmosphere and suddenly my mind is flooded with these sights, smells, and sounds of childhood experiences, rituals, and customs. I sometimes find myself muttering half-remembered fragments of prayers under my breath, or various bits of the mass that we recited with the same automaticity as the poems we learned by heart at school, and thinking of how narrowly my horizon hooped around me during my childhood – the hills around our family home, the valley weaving its verdant way down from the elevated bowl our house is nestled in, the primary school, the shop with petrol pumps across the road from Vaughan's Pub, the dark, dank Post-Office with its high counter and pockmarked sponge for wetting stamps, the hurling pitch, the Dispensary, the church and graveyard, the church bells that sounded out their doleful reminders on the half hour and hour throughout the day, the handball alley, the village hall, the shallow river – wide in places making it easy to ford.[5] These few square miles were the extent of my world for the most part, and there was a mixture of adventure and apprehension any time we ventured beyond those local borders to exotic, far-flung regions where my relatives lived – effectively other parts of the same province in the south west of Ireland. On Sundays, we sometimes rushed out of eleven o'clock mass early (or skipped it altogether – my family were not especially devout) in a frantic dash to make the first point-to-point[6] – the names of each of those point-to-point venues transport me back any time I see them on a signpost or map – the names reel past along with images, sounds, and smells that are often quite vivid. On those Sundays, in the South, it felt as though I was briefly orbiting around a world with its own significance – familiar yet foreign – a place where different co-ordinates dictated movement and under-standing. It was not quite *my* home, but one to which I felt some sort of gravitational pull all the same. As time went on, I realised that I belonged to both of these worlds, even if one was more 'home' than the other, until one day I no longer lived in Ireland, and they began to merge into one large 'place' that I called 'home'. I often feel as though these places call to me; they make demands of a sort; they solicit gestures of commitment and allegiance. I feel obliged in certain ways – though it might be difficult to articulate exactly what

---

[5] Broadford is a compound based on a literal translation of the original Irish name – *Áth* (Ford) *Leathan* (Broad/Wide). Running through the middle of the village is the O'Garney river with a wide, shallow ford 'where people travelling from East Clare were able to cross the O'Garney river on their way through the two passes in the Slieve Bearnagh Mountains before heading Southwards to Limerick or Eastwards to Killaloe' (see www.clarelibrary.ie/eolas/coclare/heri-tage/pdfs/broadford.pdf). The village is described as 'nestled' in the Glenomra valley. Glenomra is most likely the anglicised compound of Gleann (glen) and Ómra (amber). The area was known then as the amber glen: "Glemomra, the amber valley, gets its name from the distinctive colouring revealed as the rays of the sinking sun catches [sic] the heather clad hillside". (see Pat O'Brien, 2022: 11). My family home is in the townland of Muingboy, about a mile and a half from the village on the road to Limerick. The original Irish name would have been *An* (The) *Mhoing* (Fen) *Bhuí* (Yellow) – the yellow fen.

[6] Point-to-Points are a type of steeplechase that date back to a match race in North Cork in 1752 when Cornelius O'Callaghan and Edmund Blake raced each other on horseback between the Church steeples in Doneraile and Buttevant. Point-to-Points evolved into three-mile races around a circuit with fences, where young National Hunt horses are introduced to the sport and ridden by amateur jockeys. My father's side of the family has been breeding and training thoroughbred horses for almost a century.

those demands are and how they are relevant for what we might think of as 'ethics'. Seamus Heaney evokes something of this when he describes the recognition and pull of allegiance (something which he is at once compelled and repelled by) when reflecting on the persecution of young Catholic women, punished by their neighbours for consorting with English soldiers in Northern Ireland during the Troubles. He confesses that he

> would connive
> in civilized outrage
> yet understand the exact
> and tribal, intimate revenge. (Heaney, 2018: 42)

I am quite certain that Heidegger was *profoundly* concerned with these elements of our historical situatedness. That is not to say that Heidegger thinks that we should begin issuing rules and directives based on local prejudices. Nevertheless, to think historically means to understand how things come to be meaningful for us as people who are *bound* in certain ways and that this can and/ or should inform how we might think of being bound ethically, how we might have an ethos. As we shall see in what follows, Heidegger rejects conventional forms of morality owing, among other things, to their non-situated ahistorical-ity, and their reliance on metaphysical presuppositions that he wants to resist. Instead, for Heidegger, our historical situatedness is key to identifying how we can feel bound or obliged as ethical beings.

Now, we have to proceed with caution here, and this is something that has been flagged repeatedly. We find a version of the relevant concern addressed in the 'exchanges' between Peter Singer and Bernard Williams on the question of speciesism and the notion of a human prejudice. Group membership, and the sense of commitment that such 'belonging' can issue in, has been the cause of a great deal of cruelty and persecution – not least as a result of the exclusionary convictions it can issue in. How far can we (i.e., should we) leverage cherished 'differences' in the service of our political or ethical views? What kind of relationship should obtain between our sense of belonging and ethics to begin with? For all that, as Williams points out, we have to think carefully about where and how our moral commitments and intuitions arise. Demanding that they stem from an ahistorical perspective, that of an ideal observer, for instance, might well, as Williams memorably quips in a well-known talk at Princeton University, be more inhumane and nightmarish than those injustices and horrors such absolutist principles and perspectives would have us avoid. I take this to be part of Plato's cautionary lesson in *Republic*. If we strip away the very features of human existence that make us human to begin with, in the hope of eradicating any partiality, bias, or injustice, then the cure can quickly become worse than the disease.[7]

Heidegger presents us with quite the tangle when it comes to these questions. He certainly wants to insist on the specificity and situatedness of Dasein and how they shape and determine what it is for us to be human and to belong to historical communities with their shared values and identities. Indeed, he clearly tries to conjure up, for a time, something like an exclusionary politics on that basis. And yet, we can see very clearly in his Bremen lectures that precisely the same conditions that render us historically specific and human, all too human, are the very conditions he invokes to condemn strategies of exclusion, persecution, in short, dehumanisation.[8] It would be too quick to say that we can derive a principle or set of concrete norms on that basis. Indeed, Heidegger would resist any such proposal. That would be to succumb to forms of universalism and value thinking that prevent us from taking ownership and responsibility for specific situations. Even so, I think there is certainly something to the idea that to ignore our essence as human beings, something that Heidegger laments again and again (not least in his famous letter on the question of humanism), is to ignore our ethical bond. Perhaps the most that we can hope for from Heidegger is some help in sketching the outlines of what we might call an originary and preparatory ethics, but that is not a trivial result.

According to the story recounted by Mueller that we alluded to earlier, he reports that

> on hikes, whenever they came to a church or a chapel, Heidegger always dipped his finger in the stoup and genuflected. On one occasion he [Mueller] had asked him if this was not inconsistent, since he had distanced himself from the dogma of the Church. Heidegger's answer had been: 'One must think historically. And where there has been so much praying, there the divine is present in a very special way.' (Safranski, 1998: 432–433)

This passage captures nicely just how Heidegger thinks communities can have a shared sense of what matters, where commitments might come from, and how they might have traction for us – as opposed to abstract, ungrounded imperatives plucked from the ether.[9]

---

[7] For a brief discussion of this interpretation of Plato, see O'Brien (2021).

[8] For a detailed discussion of this point, see O'Brien (2022). We also discuss it briefly in Section 2.

[9] As Vogel argues, the attempt to act according to such 'timeless' principles is, in itself, a kind of failure to face one's authentic moral situation for Heidegger (see Vogel, 1994: 19–20). Again, there is a link here to Williams' pointed response at the end of his address at the Centre for Human Values in Princeton. An audience member asks what it might be for someone to "act inhumanly". "What is it that they've lost or what is it that they've become, because they have not become an alien?" Williams' response bears reproducing in its entirety: "that's right, that's a very, very good question and I think there are a lot of complex answers to it ... when they behave inhumanly

Some commentators are keen to exploit these sporadic instances of terms like 'divine' to impute to Heidegger a religious mysticism or theological outlook. However, to read Heidegger as straightforwardly theological or mystical in this way is a failure to think through how Heidegger uses these terms. Heidegger's invocations of awe and wonder, for example, are really just the flip side of the angst we sometimes experience when meditating on the *Abgrund* that lurks behind all meaningfulness. Each instance of meaningfulness is shot through with utter meaninglessness, the nothingness which sits on the other side of meaning, everything pointing towards, ultimately, our own non-existence and loss of meaning at some point in the future. There is no divine principle understood as 'constant', vouching safe our meaningful existence, any more than there are the metaphysical constants dreamt up by Aristotle or Kant according to which we can secure our understanding of things. Indeed, as Heidegger makes clear in "Letter on Humanism", the very notion of god as first cause is itself an achievement of subjectivity and the metaphysics of presence since it begins with things that are present/extant and then simply posits the cause of everything present/extant/actual as the ultimate source or cause of these created things. To think through what terms like 'god' or 'divine' might truly mean requires that we forgo this kind of thinking, that we think properly about being and the nothing.

Part of how meaningfulness, our 'sense' of the 'real', emerges in the first place is itself, if we pay close attention, run through with the meaninglessness around it, the yawning abyss of nothingness which sits either side of any moment of it. Heidegger describes us as the 'null basis of a nullity', and each 'occasion', each meaningful moment of our lives, takes place against the backdrop of our own future non-existence (i.e., meaninglessness) and is prefigured by the nothingness, the abyssal, the meaninglessness that precedes it and will come after it. This is enough to inspire the dread and awe that have long been associated with religious experience in the past, but Heidegger's thought is no latter-day mysticism. Even when requesting a Catholic funeral service and burial, Heidegger was not, I believe, thinking in terms of religion but, rather, he was, as the passage above indicates, thinking 'historically'. He was submitting himself to and being reclaimed by the 'place', the 'ground' from which his own sense of self, in part, emerged. As Safranski recounts:

In January 1976 Heidegger requested that his Messkirch compatriot, the Freiburg professor of theology Bernhard Welte, visit him for a talk. He

---

(interesting, as you rightly say, it doesn't mean that they act like an animal, for instance they don't destroy something in rage), typically, if they act inhumanly, what they typically do is that they behave either like a machine or a disembodied intelligence. And, one way of acting inhumanly is to act on certain kinds of principles" (Bernard Williams, 2002). Hatab offers a similar criticism of traditional moral theories (see Hatab, 2000: 62).

informed him that, when the time came, he would like to be buried in Messkirch cemetery. He asked for a Church funeral and for Welte to speak at his graveside. This last conversation between the two men centred on the experience that proximity of death included within itself proximity to one's native soil. 'Floating in the room,' Welte reported, 'was also Eckhart's idea that God equalled Nothingness.' (Safranski, 1998: 432)

Safranski goes on to quote from what is apparently Heidegger's 'last utterance in his own hand' – a greeting to Welte on May 22:

> Cordial greetings to the new honorary citizen of their common hometown Messkirch – Bernhard Welte – from an older one …May this feastday of homage be joyful and life-giving. May the contemplative spirit of all participants be unanimous. For there is need for contemplation whether and how, in the age of uniform technological world civilization, there can still be such a thing as home. (Safranski, 1998: 432)

Even in his very last days, two days before his death in fact, Heidegger was still thinking of how we should respond to the levelling effects of *Gestell* in the technological age, which erases all difference, equalising everyone and everything. In such a predicament, the same predicament that urgently requires that we think carefully about the 'ethical bond' (as we shall see below), he asks whether there 'can still be such a thing as home'.[10] How are we to be at home, to find an 'abode', to dwell, that is, have an 'ethos', in such a world?

Heidegger wants us to see how our 'history', bounded as it is by finitude and thus nothingness, is, to various degrees, constitutive of how our lives matter and how things are meaningful. This will not give us a *vade mecum* – it will not immediately issue in specific norms. However, that is not to say that it is not relevant to thinking about what it means to be a human being and what it might be to think ethically. We might, to be sure, still find ourselves in something of a bind, since Heidegger consistently looks to resist all universalism, which he sees as a kind of hangover of the metaphysical thinking he wishes to overcome. However, what he never appears to have quite worked out for himself is just how to deal with the fact that the background conditions which are operative in terms of us finding ourselves to be thrown, historical, radically finite, radically contingent beings, do appear to obtain universally. Indeed, they motivate his own condemnation of the treatment of persecuted people as a violation of their humanity. At the same time, it would be

---

[10] Rather than opt for one of the various contested translations of the term *Gestell*, I have elected to leave it in the German for the most part. I have always favoured the slightly awkward translation 'Enframing'. However, this has the disadvantage of missing the various ways that Heidegger riffs on the root "*stellen*". The desire to retain those resonances in Heidegger's discussions of the essence of technology is part of the reason that "positionality" or "imposition" is looked on more favourably in recent scholarship.

misleading to suggest that by 'background conditions' Heidegger is thinking of something like transcendental subjectivity. Nothingness and the interplay of presence and absence are not universal or transcendental in that way; there is no constant underlying metaphysical principle at work. Nevertheless, Heidegger insists, what we 'share' is a failure to successfully think through what we mean by being and nothingness. And, even though we approach this question as human beings who are grounded in specific places and times, the question itself (and thus our essence as human beings) is *the same.*[11]

"Letter on Humanism" and the Ethical Bond

Specialists and non-specialists alike often assume that Heidegger dismissed the very possibility of ethics.[12] Readers might wonder then as to whether we are on something of a fool's errand scouring through Heidegger's philosophy looking for ethical views or a thinking that could inform or contribute to ethics. However, a close reading of Heidegger's well-known settling of accounts with Sartre, existentialism, Marxism, Christianity, as well as Roman and Renaissance humanism ("Letter on Humanism") shows that his treatment of the notion of ethics is not nearly so straightforwardly negative as is sometimes supposed. What we find, in fact, is quite a careful and nuanced discussion of the relevance of his thinking for what it might be to approach the dual questions of humanism and ethics.

Heidegger's "Letter on Humanism" is an important document in terms of understanding the development of his thinking. It offers important clarifications on what he may have meant by the notion of 'the turn' (*die Kehre*), on how his thinking diverged from some key principles of Sartre's existentialism, on the continuing relevance of *Being and Time* and the questions he addressed in that work, on why he was *not* anti-humanist, along with what he saw as problematic about conventional approaches to morality and/or value thinking commonly construed. Without straying too far away from our central topic, it's worth mentioning that this text repays a careful rereading if only to dispel the misguided view that 'the turn' signals a 'turn away' from what he took to be the dead-born project of *Being and Time* in favour of a different project in his later work.[13] Heidegger could hardly have been more explicit that that is *not*

---

[11] We shall leave to one side here the fraught issue of whether Heidegger's account of the essence of the human being involves retaining notions of disclosure which are not in themselves subject to change but rather issue in different specific temporal situations

[12] Lauren Freeman lists several of the better-known exponents of this view from among the "first generation" of Heidegger interpreters in her helpful overview of the treatment of the topic of ethics in Heidegger scholarship (see Freeman, 2010). We will look at some more recent examples of this view in Section 3.

[13] Olafson, for instance, offers a rather crude version of this view. (See Section 3.) In other work I have referred to this view as 'the discontinuity thesis'. See O'Brien (2013).

what he meant by the notion of 'the turn' and that *Being and Time* remained a touchstone for all of his later thought. He underlines again in this essay the fundamental continuity of his thinking from *Being and Time* onwards but also, crucially, he discusses how his own thinking is relevant to questions concerning how we should live and what he takes the very notion of ethics to mean.

In response to Beaufret's question concerning the need for ontology to be supplemented by ethics, Heidegger relates a story concerning an acquaintance who wondered when he was going to write an ethics and offers a sustained meditation on the question of ethics that spans the final pages of the essay. When we consider how Heidegger responds to Beaufret and the anecdote recounted, it is remarkable that so many people still assume that Heidegger's views on ethics are entirely dismissive:

> Soon after *Being and Time* appeared a young friend asked me, "When are you going to write an ethics?" Where the essence of the human being is thought so essentially, i.e., solely from the question concerning the truth of being, and yet without elevating the human being to the center of beings, a longing necessarily awakens for a peremptory directive and for rules that say how the human being, experienced from ek-sistence toward being, ought to live in a fitting manner. The desire for an ethics presses ever more ardently for fulfillment as the obvious no less than the hidden perplexity of human beings soars to immeasurable heights. The greatest care must be fostered upon the ethical bond at a time when technological human beings, delivered over to mass society, can attain reliable constancy only by gathering and ordering all their plans and activities in a way that corresponds to technology. (GA9: 352–353/268. Emphasis added)

The question concerning the *meaning* of being ignited a lifelong philosophical project for Heidegger; and the being of the human being remains essential to that undertaking (contrary to what advocates of the discontinuity thesis suppose). In terms of the claim that this letter itself is a statement of Heidegger's abjuration of the project undertaken in *Being and Time* in favour of his subsequent efforts to seek the truth of being, he again undermines the plausibility of that thesis since what he is concerned with is to think the "essence of the human being . . . essentially, i.e., solely from the question concerning the truth of being, and yet without elevating the human being to the center of beings". However, not elevating the human being to the 'center of beings' is not to disregard Dasein or the human being in favour of the truth of being altogether. That was never what Heidegger suggested or intended. What Heidegger further suggests is that the need to revisit the very possibility of ethics presses upon us *all the more urgently* in the technological age, an age where we are faced with unprecedented challenges in terms of the influence of mass society and *Gestell*. It is difficult to reconcile what Heidegger states here with the view that he dismissed the very possibility of engaging with ethical questions. By 'ethical bond', Heidegger clearly does not mean a series of concrete rules to govern conduct and regulate our lives. He is thinking at a more originary[14] level as to how we should think of ethos, a way to be and live that is consistent with our essence as human beings. Heidegger's criticisms of conventional morality, as his comments concerning the need to carefully attend to the question of our ethical bond show, should not be understood as an eschewal of the very possibility of ethical thinking. Ethics has traditionally involved the search for a first principle of some kind (e.g., the categorical imperative, the greatest happiness principle) and/or a source for our moral obligations (e.g., divine command, the state). These approaches do not begin with or recognise the importance of the essence of the human being (as Heidegger conceives it) and are therefore to be resisted. We cannot begin to think ethically, for Heidegger, until we have first considered the essence of the human being, and this necessitates that we think outside of the metaphysics of presence, which has failed to ask the being question and relies on a sense of beings as a whole that Heidegger vigorously resists. The source and force of our ethical bond relate to how things matter to us as human beings. And, in seeing how meaning and significance emerge for us in our own lives, by considering our essence as human beings, Heidegger is shining a light on how we feel the pull of recognition and obligation to others who we see as people who are grounded in a world that emerges as meaningful and significant in the same way. We are exhorted to acknowledge the dignity of human beings as 'siblings'[15] standing out into the nameless and experiencing and valuing their lives, projects, relationships and 'home' against that backdrop. This avoids the neutralising indifference of a categorical rule and thus the possibility of an ethics of the inhumane. It further acknowledges how traditions and values emerge in specific contexts, which cannot be accounted for from a context-free, ahistorical perspective. Our 'situation' needs to be recognised as playing a crucial role in how we feel commitments and obligations.

Heidegger begins his essay on humanism with a discussion of one of Beaufret's questions that most people are by now familiar with: how are we to restore some sense or meaning to the word 'humanism'? And, as the essay unfolds as an extended answer to this and other questions attributed to Beaufret, we note that the supposedly pejorative remarks concerning ethics are in fact very heavily qualified. Heidegger is critical of the various 'isms' of his day

---

[14] The term 'originary' will, for some readers, prompt immediate associations with Nancy. The interpretation of "Letter on Humanism" offered below intersects with Nancy's discussion in "Heidegger's 'Originary Ethics'" at times. However, Nancy's emphasis is not quite the same as ours and his treatment in that essay is very much preliminary. See Nancy (2002).

[15] See Caputo (1987: 205, 259).

(including Marxism and existentialism); he is similarly wary of the fact that ethics, logic and metaphysics, as they currently hold sway, emerged in and belong to the realm of public opinion, the marketplace of ideas, which he is very much critical of.

Nevertheless, these critical remarks hardly deny the very possibility of ethics – rather one has to ask the question concerning the meaning of being, if not before, then at least in tandem with the question concerning our ethical bond. Conventional morality has already assumed something about beings as a whole which betrays a failure to account for what distinguishes human beings, namely, *their* capacity to distinguish between being and beings, to realise that being itself is not a thing and is thus no-thing, i.e., nothing. To that extent Heidegger believes that conventional morality and other forms of humanism (including existentialism and Marxism) are metaphysically the same insofar as they share fundamental presuppositions about the meaning of being which amount to a failure to properly think through or ask the being question and what it entails in terms of the meaning of human being.[16] Existentialism, for instance, adheres to a Cartesian subjectivity that Heidegger rejects. Everything in turn is understood as somehow the achievement of the subjectivity of the subject, and the extreme existentialist vision of human freedom that Heidegger rails against emerges in this context. Even when it comes to the notion of God (e.g., as *prima causa*), we again begin with constantly present, actual things. God is then thought simply as a cause of things taken to be actual and present without ever wondering about the notion of the being of those things thought to be in being, or the being of god itself. This, for Heidegger, simply reduces the notion of god to an object of our 'reckoning' and our causal reasoning. In asking the Leibnizian question of beings and nothing (Heidegger's version of the question reads: "Why are there beings at all instead of nothing?" [GA40: 1]), we fail to see that we have yet to consider the notion of being itself and/or the notion of nothing as something other than the negation of some present thing.

Heidegger's thinking is often characterised as anti-humanist. Indeed, Vogel, while trying to reconstruct what he takes to be a positive account of morality or ethics, insists that his reconstruction necessitates that we think with Heidegger *against* Heidegger. Vogel frames his reconstruction in this quasi-adversarial way as a result of the pejorative nature of remarks that Heidegger makes about conventional morality in *Being and Time*. Heidegger makes similar observations in "Letter on 'Humanism'":

> True, '-isms' have for a long time now been suspect. But the market of public opinion continually demands new ones. We are always prepared to supply the demand. Even such names as 'logic,' 'ethics,' and 'physics' begin to flourish

---

[16] See GA9: 321/245).

> only when originary thinking comes to an end … The dominance of such terms ['isms'] is not accidental. It rests above all in the modern age upon the peculiar dictatorship of the public realm. (GA9: 315– 317/241–242)

Heidegger is concerned here with what he takes to be superficial forms of ethics and humanism. He is interested instead in rethinking the idea of being ethically bound and our essence as human beings in the context of the truth of being. He is not trying to disqualify the very possibility of ethics from the outset.

Heidegger next begins to weave his concerns with language into the essay and goes on to bemoan the debasement and decline of language, which "arises from a threat to the essence of humanity" (GA9: 318/243). Thinking, language, the question of being, and its relation to our essence as human beings, all emerge jointly as part of Heidegger's concerns, clearly giving the lie to the idea that the truth of being is thought at the expense of what Heidegger deemed to be the excessively 'Dasein-centric' or overly subjectivist approach of *Being and Time*. He argues that

> under the dominance of the modern metaphysics of subjectivity [language] almost irremediably falls out of its element. Language still denies us its essence: that it is the house of the truth of being. Instead, language surrenders itself to our mere willing and trafficking as an instrument of domination over beings. Beings themselves appear as actualities in the interaction of cause and effect. We encounter beings as actualities in a calculative businesslike way, but also scientifically and by way of philosophy, with explanations and proofs … But if the human being is to find his way once again into the nearness of being he [the human being] must first learn to exist in the nameless. (GA9: 318–319/243. Emphasis added)

Heidegger exhorts us to learn to exist in the "nameless". This, at first, may seem like a rather cryptic remark. However, to be nameless, to be without name, is to be without meaning, that which is not meaningfully present, the abyss which is the correlate of any emergence of meaningful presence. This is the self-effacing backdrop against which meaning emerges in Heidegger's view, that is, against the backdrop of the nothing and nowhere. Adding further weight to the claim that Heidegger is not anti-humanist, he insists that human beings must let themselves be "claimed again by being". We need to see language and meaning as emerging from *this* 'claim', affording us a home to dwell in "the truth of being". With explicit reference to the analysis of care in *Being and Time*, he argues that in this 'claim', and in helping to ready human beings for this claim, there is "implied a concern about human beings". The notion of 'care' is concerned with bringing human beings back to their essence.

> What else does that in turn betoken but that man (*homo*) become human (*humanus*)? Thus *humanitas* really does remain the concern of such

> thinking. For this is humanism: meditating and caring that human beings be human and not inhumane, 'inhuman,' that is, outside their essence. But in what does the humanity of the human being consist? It lies in his essence. (GA9: 319/243–244)

Heidegger is at pains again to distance his understanding of humanism from some of the traditional forms of humanism. His point here echoes the qualifications he made concerning conventional morality. Humanism as simply another 'ism' is something Heidegger disavows, but that is not to say that he is advocating the inhumane. Rather, Heidegger insists that all previous forms of humanism operate with "an already established interpretation of nature, history, world, and the ground of world, that is, of beings as a whole". Any attempt to determine the essence of the human being "that already presupposes an interpretation of beings without asking about the truth of being, whether knowingly or not, is metaphysical" (GA9: 321/245). The point is a familiar one. Humanism, in all of its forms hitherto, has failed to ask the question concerning the meaning of being. It presupposes that the meaning of being is self-evident and thus unquestioningly both perpetuates and operates within the ambit of the metaphysics of presence. Heidegger makes the further point that because these metaphysical humanisms do not consider how the human being essentially belongs to the truth of being, they fail to think properly the being of the human being. Instead, they tend to look on the human being as one particular being among others and, indeed, from the perspective of animality, as a rational animal, a bio-anthropological entity with 'properties' like 'reason' or 'logos'. By contrast, Heidegger questions whether the essence of the human being lies in animality at all.[17] To think of human beings in terms of animalitas (instead of humanitas) is, Heidegger adds, to think metaphysically. In this way metaphysics closes itself from the simple essential fact that human beings occur in their essence only where they are claimed by being. Heidegger insists that previous attempts to deal with the human being operate with the same metaphysical presuppositions and fail to touch on the essence of the human being. And, the essence of the human being lies in its 'ek-sistence', a claim that Heidegger traces back to *Being and Time* and reaffirms here. By hyphenating terms and alternating the spelling (ex-ist/ek-sist) Heidegger is signalling the etymology of the word 'exist'. The Latin origin of the word exist is 'ex(s)istere', which means "to stand out, be perceptible, hence to exist, f. *ex*- out + *sistere* reduplicated form of *sta*- to stand".[18] (He sometimes uses the Greek prefix 'ek', which also means 'out of'.) Ek-sisting or Existing, for Heidegger, is a standing-out of or from and is to be distinguished from the

---

[17] See GA9: 322–323/246–247.

[18] See *The Compact Edition of the Oxford English Dictionary* (1979), 926.

traditional notion of 'existentia'. A way to render this somewhat idiomatically in English is to describe Dasein as the 'out-standing' being. He had looked to clarify this again in the *Beiträge* in the 1930s and it is crucial to an understanding of *Being and Time* as well: "ek-sistence thought in this way is not identical with the traditional concept of *existentia*, which means actuality in contrast to the meaning of *essentia* as possibility" (GA9: 325/248). Note again that Heidegger invokes an earlier discussion in *Being and Time*, this time where he emphasised that the 'essence' of Dasein "lies in its existence", insisting that he is not concerned with the "opposition between *existentia* and *essentia*" since "neither of these metaphysical determinations of being, let alone their relationship, is yet in question". Neither is this a "universal statement about *Dasein*" as a traditional "name for 'object,' intending to express the metaphysical concept of the actuality of the actual". Rather, for Heidegger, the claim is that the human being *is* in such a way that they are "the 'there' [*das 'Da'*], that is, the clearing of being" (GA9: 325/248). Heidegger is keen to move us away from the idea that we are simply one living creature among others. True, "plants and animals are lodged in their respective environments", but that is not to say that they "are placed freely into the clearing of being which alone is 'world,' they lack language".[19] This involves a very particular conception of language, however, one peculiar to Dasein. Language is not simply "the utterance of an organism" or "the expression of a living *thing*". It is not to be thought of (essentially) as a collection of symbols or "even in terms of the character of signification". Rather, language is to be understood as "the clearing-concealing advent of being itself" (GA9: 326/248–249).

Again, it's important to bear in mind that Heidegger is trying to answer the question as to the essence of the human being. The human being 'ek-sists', that is to say, we live towards the future – we stand out into the 'not now'. We ourselves *are* as an interplay of presence and absence, and meaningfulness emerges for us as beings who are thrown into historical worlds set against the nothing and nowhere. We are not ourselves constantly statically present; we are not objects or things that can be understood as actual in that way. As 'there', we are not present in the way that a table might be thought to be 'actually' there in front of us. Indeed, the table itself is not really 'there' in the way that the tradition has suggested either; it is rather the table that we intend and is itself in terms of its possibilities, its meaningful presence is not exhausted in actuality.[20] We are rather a dynamic, ecstatic awareness, and allow things to emerge as

---

[19] Heidegger meditates on the question concerning the essential differences between Dasein and animals in numerous texts, most notably perhaps in *Fundamental Concepts of Metaphysics* and the *Bremen Lectures*. He returns to this issue again in the *Zollikon Seminars* (see Heidegger, 1987: 306–307/243–244).

[20] See Section 2 for a more extensive discussion of 'things'.

meaningfully present in historical contexts in ways that exceed the notion of pure presence. When Heidegger writes the 'the human being ek-sists', as he explains again here, he is not answering a question as to "whether the human being actually is or not".[21] Rather he is saying something about the essence of the human being:

> As ek-sisting, the human being sustains Da-sein in that he takes the *Da*, the clearing of being, into 'care.' But Da-sein itself occurs essentially as 'thrown.' It unfolds in the throw of being as a destinal sending. (GA9: 326–327/249)

Let's try to unpack some of this, since at times it can appear as though Heidegger simply states and restates ideas in variations of his own unique idiolect. For one thing, Heidegger is certainly *not* anti-humanist or inimical to the very possibility of ethics. Rather, what he is trying to determine is how we might first think of something like ethical obligation that accords with *our essence as human beings*, which in turn is to realise that our thrownness into historical, meaningful times and places occurs against the constant backdrop of self-concealing, abyssal nothingness. To be 'ecstatic' (*Ecstasis/Ekstase*), to 'ek-sist' (how we are essentially), is (literally) to *not* be 'static'; rather, we 'stand out' (into the nothing). We are never present or actual in the way the tradition might have us think. We are more than what appears as actually present at any given moment; we are out beyond the present, with the shadow of our past hovering, as we lurch forward towards and anticipate the future. There is always something outstanding for Dasein and we in turn are 'out-standing' beings. We 'are' as beings that are 'towards', we are ourselves a constant interplay of presence and absence. Our experience is always tinged with an awareness of the finitude that runs through the emergence of meaningful presence for us. What it means for us to be and the source of meaningfulness and significance, the way things both mean something and matter to us is shaped by how we ourselves are as a clearing for the emergence of meaningfulness, our irreducibility to any idea of a moment that might capture us in our totality – a fantasy of eternal or constant presence. We find meaning, meaning finds us, as identities that are not reducible to the present or actual, but that constantly stand out into the nothing and the nameless.

The foregoing considerations have further particular implications for how we think of ourselves as the beings that have language. Instead of construing human beings simply as living creatures who possess language along with other capacities, Heidegger regards language as "the house of being in which the human ek-sists by dwelling, in that he belongs to the truth of being, guarding it"

---

[21] Heidegger again frames his current views on humanism and the challenges we face in the context of what he had introduced first in *Being and Time*. See GA9: 332–333/253.

(GA9: 333/254). Meaningfulness, the linguistic utterance, word – these always bear the trace of more than what they ostensibly signify, and they carry the silent echo of that in the face of which they emerge. They point to the ineffable and remind us of the fact that impermanence, void, or absence (in short – the abyssal) is the constant correlate of any occasion or event of meaningfulness. Meaningfulness can only be understood as emerging from out of concealedness and meaninglessness. There is no permanent principle underlying all accidents and contingency, no constant in view of which we understand change or make sense of things. To say that something 'is' is not to say that it is simply present understood as fully actualised.

Heidegger has gone to some lengths in previous work to demonstrate that the notion of being as constant presence belongs to a metaphysics that he is trying to overcome. He underlines again the importance of recognising the ontological difference, that is, that "being 'is' precisely not 'a being'" (GA9: 334–335/254–255). The consequence of not keeping this in view is that "being is all too easily represented as a 'being' after the fashion of the familiar sorts of beings that act as causes and are actualized as effects" (GA9: 334–335/254–255). Heidegger complains, and not for the first time, that the implications of his claims to this effect in *Being and Time* and elsewhere were misunderstood, leading to the belief that "the attempt in *Being and Time* ended in a blind alley" when, in fact, "the thinking that hazards a few steps in *Being and Time* has even today not advanced beyond that publication" (GA9: 343/261). That is not to say that there is no progress or that his thinking hasn't evolved, but his project revolves around an attempt to make clear what he was first approaching in *Being and Time*. What he didn't quite manage at that time was to allow "the truth of being come to language and that thinking attain to this language" (GA9: 343/261). He repeats what he takes to be a shortcoming in his own earlier efforts towards the end of the essay. He had held back the third division of part one of *Being and Time*; at the time of publication, he had not as yet found a way to proceed without the aid of the language of metaphysics (metaphysics of presence), which made it difficult to avoid misinterpretations (GA9: 327–328/249–250). What we begin to see more clearly now is that Heidegger conceives of his project in *Being and Time* as directly related to the attempt here to articulate a non-metaphysical humanism. Originary ethics then *is* related to the very core of his thinking.

Heidegger is trying to articulate something fundamental, in a way – simple, but which evades description in our ordinary language. When we think of anything emerging for us as meaningfully present, when we say that something 'is' in that context, what do we mean by 'is'? Heidegger teases out the questions of being and nothingness that he had famously raised in the 1929 inaugural lecture. He remains adamant that nothingness is not derived from the 'not' of negation since that negation is a negation of something already taken to be present, to be actual, to be the case. But beyond presence there is absence that is not the negation of something already present. How do we express this 'nihilation'? It is not the negation of being understood as something present. Moreover, being is not itself 'a being', and therefore is not itself some-thing, any-thing, it is not itself 'a thing' and is therefore 'no-thing'. We ourselves are as the beings that 'stand-out' into the nothing, we are ec-static, ek-sistent. Nothing, as Heidegger understands it here, does not annul something already taken to be present.

But how do we find a way to express this? We are truly here in the domain of the nameless, the abyssal. How does language emerge from the wordless, the nameless? We 'are', essentially, only in so far as we have recognised ourselves as the beings that stand out into the nothing. We are, furthermore, beings that are thrown into historical epochs where meaningfulness is ordained in accordance with the specific destinal sending of our day. (We will discuss this in more detail in the section that follows.) To live in the light of this awareness is key to understanding how we come to be bound ethically. This may seem excessively vague and underdetermined to some readers, but this is ultimately where we need to begin according to Heidegger. In thinking of nothingness in this context, the domain of the nameless, we enter that region where we can genuinely think about the nature of God, divinity, the holy – notions understood in the historical sense invoked by Heidegger in his response to Max Mueller (Safranski, 1998: 432–433). He fulminates against ideas such as God as the highest value since that is to think of God in such a way that it becomes an achievement of subjectivity rather than as a notion that resists any attempt to turn it into an object of our 'reckoning', something that we can 'calculate'.[22] Here and elsewhere he criticises the idea of God as first cause.[23] The metaphysically couched language of the tradition remains a necessary starting point – we cannot begin from 'nowhere'. Nevertheless, Heidegger rues the fact that, even though he repeatedly highlighted his use of terms in very specific and particular ways, he failed to make clear that he was not trying to operate from within the confines of traditional metaphysics. In *Being and Time* he is trying to make its themes understandable for existing philosophy but believed that that was possible "only within the horizon of that existing philosophy and the use of its current terms" (GA9: 357/271). He subsequently came to realise that the use of

---

[22] Heidegger frequently distinguishes between two types of thinking: calculative thinking (das rechnende Denken) and meditative thinking (*das besinnliche Nachdenken*): "*So gibt es den zwei Arten von Denken, die beide jeweils auf ihre Weise berechtigt und nötig sind: das rechnende Denken und das besinnliche Nachdenken*" (Heidegger, 2015: 13).

[23] See GA9: 180–182/266–267.

traditional conceptual language was doomed to fail. Readers approached the key questions "according to the established terminology in its customary meaning" (GA9: 357/271). Thus, Heidegger's attempts to think through a non-metaphysical humanism are not reducible to ethics and ontology ordinarily construed. However, that is not to say that Heidegger disallows the very possibility of ethical thinking any more than he thinks that one cannot undertake ontological inquiry. Rather, what is needed is a new approach. Furthermore, Heidegger's approach to the most basic of ontological questions has ethical implications, since it concerns what it means for the human being to be and the essence of the human being. Living in accordance with our essence as human beings is, Heidegger believes, an ethical enterprise. Meditating on ontology and ethics, Heidegger resists the traditional notions in order to avoid the pitfalls of using metaphysically 'loaded' concepts (as he had done in *Being and Time*). But that is not to say that Heidegger favours what he calls here the 'valueless', the 'inhumane', or 'irrationalism'. The conventional ways that values, humanism, and logic or reason have been handled by the tradition have failed to ask the more originary question that concerns Heidegger; they share presuppositions that Heidegger is not willing to grant. They operate within the metaphysics of constant presence and thus block our access to the true essence of the human being and the historical worlds we reside in. In that sense, they block our access to our true abode and lead to a kind of 'homelessness'. What he means by homelessness here is related to the idea that 'dwelling' properly in our world is to live in full awareness of how we are thrown into an historical world and the nothingness that borders each emergence of historical presence, that is, the particular way that meaningfulness 'comes to pass' in any given epoch. The only constancy, in terms of how each of these epoch-defining ways through which everything emerges as meaningfully present hold sway, is the utter lack of anything underlying as constant, the nothingness that nihilates at the edges of each event or occasion. The thinking that tries to express this is not a thinking that issues in rules or directives – it is neither theoretical nor practical; instead, it "comes to pass [*ereignet sich*] before this distinction" (GA9: 358/272). Finding our essence as human beings means being able to exist once more in the 'nameless' – to see the role that absence plays in our lives, the 'nihilation' that "occurs essentially in being itself" as opposed to something that we see "in beings": "The nihilating in being is the essence of what I [Heidegger] call the nothing. Hence, because it thinks being, thinking thinks the nothing" (GA9: 360/273).

A little earlier in the essay, Heidegger briefly discusses the notion of *ethos* understood as abode. It emerges in the context of Heidegger's recounting of a story where some visitors happened upon Heraclitus engaged in the mundane activity of warming himself at his stove. Struck by their dismay at the banality of the scene, Heraclitus welcomes the passers-by into his home with the words:

"For here too the gods are present" (GA9: 355/270). Our interpretation has come full circle: when pressed by Mueller upon observing certain religious gestures at a country chapel, Heidegger explains to his companion that the divine is present in a special way in these places, where local communities gather together in the world they share. In this story, of a person warming themselves at a simple stove, 'even here':

> in that ordinary place where every thing and every circumstance, each deed and thought is intimate and commonplace, that is, familiar [*geheuer*], 'even there' in the sphere of the familiar ... it is the case that 'the gods come to presence.' ... The (familiar) abode for humans is the open region for the presencing of god **(the unfamiliar one).**'

> If the name 'ethics,' in keeping with the basic meaning of the word ἦθος, should now say that ethics ponders the abode of the human being, then that thinking which thinks the truth of being as the primordial element of the human being, as one who eksists, is in itself originary ethics. (GA9: 356–357/270–271. Emphasis Added)[24]

In this region of the familiar and the everyday, if we attend properly to how we are historically thrown into the place and time of our 'home', we can pay heed to how the familiar is prefigured by the unfamiliar, how the meaningful is prefigured by the meaningless, the named by the nameless. In the familiar, where we are surrounded by the manifold 'things' that have emerged as familiar, that is, as meaningful, we at once have a glimpse of the unfamiliar, the meaningless, the nameless, the nothing and nowhere – when such is our abode, we are truly 'at home'; here too, the gods come to presence.[25] To be at home in what is at once a site for the self-concealing revealing of 'the unhomely', to welcome the unhomely and unfamiliar, and to dwell in the interplay between the familiar and unfamiliar – that is the source of the originary ethics that Heidegger wishes us to think. Thus, to fully understand the essence of the human being is the gateway to identifying our ethical bond:

> Only so far as the human being, ek-sisting into the truth of being, belongs to being can there come from being itself the assignment of those directives that must become law and rule for human beings. In Greek to assign is *nemein*.

---

[24] Heidegger emphasises the continuity with *Being and Time* again here. See GA9: 357/271.

[25] As Heidegger explains in "The Thing" in GA79: "The divinities are the hinting messengers of godhood. From the concealed reign of these appears the god in his essence, **withdrawing from every comparison with what is present** (GA79: 17/16. Emphasis added)". 'Beckoning' would work better than 'hinting' in the first sentence quoted above. To consider the role of 'the gods' in a similar context, see the discussion of Patrick Kavanagh's poem "Epic" in Section 3 (Kavanagh, 2018: 48).

> *Nomos* is not only the law but more originally the assignment contained in the
> dispensation of being. Only this assignment is capable of enjoining humans
> into being. Only such enjoining is capable of supporting and obligating.
> Otherwise all law remains merely something fabricated by human reason.
> More essential than instituting rules is that human beings find the way to their
> abode in the truth of being . . . (GA9: 360–361/274)

Heidegger urges us to find a way to an "abode in the truth of being". In attending
to "the clearing of being", thinking "puts its saying of being into language as the
home of eksistence". As sense-making creatures, thrown into worlds where
things emerge meaningfully against the backdrop of the nothing and nowhere,
we find ourselves bound to the time and place of our own meaningful existence.
As dynamic sites for the emergence of meaning, we ourselves belong to a world
that is set against the abyssal. Heidegger's originary ethics is not a matter of
'valuing' or 'reckoning' according to the subjectivity of the subject or the
calculative reckoning of 'value thinking'. Meaning is something that happens
to and through us; our basic affectivity itself attests to our attunement to the
nothing that announces itself through each occasion of meaningful presence.
Thus, we are exhorted to become what we already are, to live in accord with our
essence, which is to exist once more in the nameless. Recognising how we
respond to the call/claim of being as our way of standing out into the nothing
and sharing in meaningful historical worlds with others (caring for ourselves
and others as co-respondents to this call/claim) is to understand what it is to be
part of a community, to be 'at home' in a world, to have an ethos, to dwell
together as a fragile community with a dignity that we share through our shared
human essence. If we *don't* begin with an understanding of our true human
essence, then our attempts to understand what it is for us to be, how and why
things matter to us, and how we feel the pull of obligations that respect and
preserve this dignity of a shared humanity are bound to go awry. Instead, we are
liable to think 'inhumanly' – for instance, according to the logic of ahistorical
principles, categorical imperatives, necessary definitions, what have you.

Many a reader is likely to conclude at this point that these considerations are all
too vague and/or hopelessly impoverished, leaving us with little to go on in terms
of helping us determine what it would be to live a good life or how this extends to
how we live together as communities and societies. We will return to this question
in more detail in what follows. For now, however, we will try to sketch something
that will hopefully seem more positive or less indeterminate than what many
interpreters of Heidegger have previously offered in this context. Heidegger
insists that we urgently need to consider how we are to be bound ethically
given the dangers of the technological age. Ethics in turn can only be addressed
from the perspective of our essence as human beings, which is something that

traditional forms of humanism and morality have failed to do. The essence of the human being is what he tries to determine during the course of his essay on humanism. Our essence lies in our 'ek-sistence'; that is, we are the beings that stand out into the nothing. How we find ourselves thrown into a particular epoch, how we find ourselves as beings-in-the-world, happens against the backdrop of the nothingness that precedes and shadows each meaningful, historical emergence for Dasein. As we shall see again in what follows, the implications of Heidegger's claims to this effect are such that our interactions with others should therefore be oriented and guided by a reverence for and recognition of how they themselves are historicised, bound and placed in similar ways – ways that give meaning and depth to our own lives, to the lives of 'our own' communities such that we find ourselves to be properly 'at home' in our worlds.

A perennial challenge for philosophers concerns the kind of footing or grounding our ethical commitments have. One way of reading Plato's dialogues is to see Plato as continually looking to subvert the Socratic (Socratic understood here as referring to the views expressed by a fictional character in the dialogues) insistence on absolute definitions (first principles) when it comes to questions concerning virtue, justice, what have you, as he tries to show us how the attempt to proceed with ethical questions as we do in geometry is destined to end in *aporia*.[26] Plato can thus be read as a critic of that kind of approach to what Aristotle in turn refers to as the 'science of human affairs'. Aristotle, for his part, insists that we cannot demand or expect the same level of precision in the science of human affairs that we expect from the exact sciences. Kant famously insisted that precisely what we need is a grounding for a metaphysics of morals so that we can rationalise our ethical lives in such a way as to be able to identify categorical (as opposed to conditional) imperatives. Nietzsche, in a stunning attack on Kantian metaphysics, ponders the challenge faced as we try to articulate ethical views without the support of a metaphysics of any kind.[27] We can think of Heidegger then as coming to this question on the back of his own attempts to revitalise the being question and to rewind back through the history of Western philosophy to the very inception of the metaphysical tradition and to think anew the joint questions of being and nothing. The despair and reactive absurdism of the existentialist response (personified by Nietzsche's madman for example[28]) ignore the possibility that meaningfulness might still emerge, even if our metaphysical constants turn out to be illusory. In terms of ethics, people can still feel obliged and dutybound despite there not being timeless laws or commandments derived from some universal reason to which everyone must submit.[29] Now

---

[26] For a discussion of this see O'Brien (2021).   [27] See Nietzsche (1974: 181–182).   [28] Ibid.
[29] Hatab summarises the issue nicely. See Hatab (2000: 55).

someone might counter that we often act as though our imperatives are unconditional. We do not take ourselves to be stating something conditional or historical, they may argue, when we say that certain things are absolutely wrong. Nevertheless, do the force of those convictions or the strength of those obligations mean that they are any less conditional, and, therefore, historical? We must not confuse the strength of our sense of obligation and compulsion with arguments for indubitable, categorical necessity. Wanting or needing something to be the case has never been an argument or reason for something being the case – desiderata are not arguments. After all, what would be considered heinous to many of us today was considered perfectly reasonable or acceptable to previous societies. Would we really want to insist that any and all of those societies were inherently morally odious or evil? We must try to understand that place and time ground us – that is part of how we are bound. We share places and times with others who are similarly bound. We are affective beings standing out into the nothing and find ourselves as thrown into these times and places. That is a key to understanding the beauty of the world we live in, how precious our times and places are, and it is the key to understanding the dignity of ourselves and other human beings. Demanding that our sense of obligation should transcend and sit outside of time, place, in short – history, is to demand too much. Indeed, to ignore the situatedness of our obligations may well result in us having to accede to views (and actions) that are patently counter-intuitive. As Williams contends, the demands imposed on us may well prove inhuman. We will continue to have disputes and dilemmas. We must allow for the fact that there will be genuine moral dilemmas and disagreements. What we need in that case is a basis for dialogue and discussion, which, if we are to go along with this reading of Heidegger, can be found in our shared essence as human beings.

2 Technology and the Ethical

Everything washes together into the uniformly distanceless ... The human does not see what for a long time now has already arrived and is occurring, and for which the atomic bomb and its explosion are merely the latest emission ... What is this clueless anxiety waiting for, if the horrible has already occurred? The horrifying is what transposes all that is out of its previous essence. What is so horrifying? It reveals and conceals itself in the way that everything presences, namely that despite all overcoming of distance, the nearness of that which is remains outstanding. (GA79: 4/4)

As we saw in the previous section, Heidegger's attempt to rethink ethics emerges in the context of his concerns with the essence of modern technology.[30] To think ethically, Heidegger insists, we need to think properly about the essence of the human being. We looked at how he undertakes as much in the "Letter on Humanism" (where those remarks are made). This work provides a useful context then for us to consider Heidegger's infamous and oft misunderstood remarks on the Holocaust in the Bremen lectures. These lectures, initially delivered in Bremen in 1949, are Heidegger's first sustained attempt to address the dangers of the modern technological age. In them, we find Heidegger returning to many of the discussions we find in the "Letter on Humanism", including, for example, an attempt to identify the essence of the human being, which is to be distinguished from the *animalitas* of the animal. Who we are and what it is for us to be "here" are gravely misunderstood when we are taken to be simply human animals, bio-anthropological entities. As Heidegger had insisted in *Being and Time*, the human being understood as Dasein can never "perish".[31] Again, in the Bremen lectures, Heidegger makes it clear that only the human being is "mortal" – only human beings are "able to die" (GA79: 17/17).[32] But Heidegger is talking about dying in the sense of being-towards-death, that is, as a being that exists towards the future, not bound to the present in the sense of actuality. Rather we are *possible* beings who are constantly making present what is absent, namely the past and the future, a future ultimately bounded by the finite limits of our own existence. We are thereby a constant interplay of presence and absence. That is part of what it is for us to be historical beings in places and times. As Heidegger argues again and again in subsequent texts, Dasein (that being that we typically designate as the human being) is not a mere animal with reason as one of its attributes. Dasein has a world, where the animal, for Heidegger, has no world.[33]

The remarks in the Bremen lectures concerning agriculture, atomic bombs, death camps, and the *non-death* of inmates in these factories of death (as we shall argue below), should be interpreted against the backdrop of Heidegger's insistence that the challenges and dangers of the technological age oblige us to return to the question of *our essence as human beings* and the related notion of an '*ethical bond*'.[34] The fact that Heidegger insists that the question of the ethical bond is directly related to the question concerning the essence of technology, and that in one of those lectures Heidegger returns to questions concerning the truth of being and the essence of the human being, lends further

---

[30] See GA9: 353/268.

[31] For an in-depth discussion of Heidegger's careful distinctions between perishing (*Verenden*), demise (*Ableben*), and dying (*sterben*) in *Being and Time* (in the context of his controversial remarks in Bremen) see O'Brien (2022).

[32] The animal, for Heidegger, can perish; perishing is something that can befall a biological creature. The human being, understood as Dasein, simply cannot 'perish'.

[33] See for example GA40: 48/47.   [34] See GA79: 27/27 and 56/53.

credibility to the view that Heidegger is attempting to think here, in part at least, ethically. Thus, his lectures on the essence of modern technology and how it threatens humanity are the obvious place to turn next.

Things *as* Things

In order to understand the way Heidegger introduces his concerns with the essence of modern technology and the dangers faced by humanity, we need to zero in on his extended meditation on the notion of the 'thing as thing' as part of the constellation of ideas that he explores. With this in mind, a brief excursus into the background to Heidegger's phenomenological approach might be of use, simply by way of orienting the reader with discussions and ideas that might otherwise appear overly abstract and/or abstruse. Heidegger's meditation on 'things' is related directly to phenomenological seeing and, in this, more than perhaps anything else, Heidegger never forswore his indebtedness to Husserl's breakthrough in terms of phenomenological 'seeing':

> access to the phenomena ... to these 'matters themselves,' called for the careful cultivation of a special kind of seeing, learning how to see things otherwise, and with attentiveness to their very mode of appearing. Genuine questioning ... arises from a confrontation with the 'matters' (*Sachen*). 'And matters are only there where there are eyes' (GA 63, 5). 'Husserl gave me my eyes,' added Heidegger, attesting to an indebtedness to Husserl, the founder of scientific phenomenology, that Heidegger would never forget. (McNeill, 2020: 1)

Seeing a thing *as* a thing remains key for Heidegger. In "Origin of the Work of Art" Heidegger explains his version of phenomenological seeing with refreshing clarity:

> We never really first perceive a throng of sensations, e.g., tones and noises, in the appearance of things – as this thing-concept alleges; rather we hear the storm whistling in the chimney, we hear the three-motored plane, we hear the Mercedes in immediate distinction from the Volkswagen. Much closer to us than all sensations are the things themselves. We hear the door shut in the house and never hear acoustical sensations or even mere sounds. In order to hear a bare sound we have to listen away from things, divert our ear from them, i.e., listen abstractly. (GA5: 10/151–152)[35]

We can already see in this perspicuous passage from the mid 1930s how Heidegger employed the phenomenological method to advance his philosophical aims. The things that 'are', their 'being', what it is that we mean when we say that there 'is', for example, a storm whistling in the chimney, or that we hear a neighbour's

---

[35] Translation from *Basic Writings*.

Mercedes in the driveway outside – does not in fact neatly reduce to the scientific account. We don't hear bare sensations. Our hearing is intentional. We 'hear', for instance, a specific car whose sound we recognise even though all that we have access to are sound waves operating on our aural apparatus. That is what Heidegger means when he says that 'the things themselves' are much closer to us 'than all sensations'. To 'experience' a 'bare' sensation, we have to move away from the experience, we have to 'abstract', to 'listen away' from 'things'. What we hear is much more than a bare sensation, we hear and see things *as* things, even though the interplay of presence and absence involved is often concealed from us as something emerges as meaningfully present within the context of the world we live in. What we mean when we see or hear some 'thing' in each of these cases, if we pay attention, goes much further than what the reductionist, scientific account of that same 'thing' or 'state of affairs' suggests. In the earlier passage, Heidegger had suggested that we need to bring the world 'near' in the 'thinging of the thing'. In other words, our capacity to see the thing *as* a thing involves the interplay of presence and absence.

Indeed, what makes any particular thing a thing is not its constant presence and actuality, or its physical composition. In a 1935 lecture course Heidegger considers the example of a nearby building; where is the 'being' of that building? What does its being consist of? The building 'is' for us in terms of its past as well as its future, its possibilities. It cannot be reduced to its actuality or some illusory notion of it being constantly present or actual, or its material composition (GA40: 25–26/35–36). This in turn points to the fact that when things emerge as meaningfully present, it always takes place within the context of the nothing and nowhere that precede and follow them. The specific way that that meaningfulness can emerge from concealedness is something that evolves and shifts from one epoch to the next in epoch-specific ways – what might be characterised as 'ordinances of revealing' or 'destinal sendings' or the 'world-ing of the world'. What remains vital is that we stay 'near' to the way the thing emerges as thing within this constant historical interplay of presence and absence and that we are not derailed by the manner in which the metaphysics of constant presence has shifted everything into the sphere of the achievement of human subjectivity and what it deems to be constantly present or its negation. Heidegger's grave concern in this series of lectures (which has profound ethical implications) is that the current way that meaningfulness emerges (as that process conceals itself – leaving us to simply see 'reality' in this 'current' way) threatens the very possibility of seeing things 'as' things any longer, threatens, that is, the possibility of any other kind of revealing and blocks us from our access to 'world'. At the same time, it bears recalling in this context that what makes us human is precisely that being, the being of things and other beings, is given to us. Hence, the inability to see things as things, in their being, keeps us removed from our essence as human beings and blocks our capacity to see humans *as* humans.

Heidegger considers the example of an empty jug in the Bremen lectures to elaborate on this insight in more detail.[36] He explains that science fails to account properly for the emptiness of the jug – the "physical sciences assure us that the jug is filled with air and with all that constitutes the compound mixture of air" (GA79: 8–9/8–9). Heidegger's point is quite a simple one. Nevertheless, once one grasps his insight in the context of his concerns with the influence of a certain kind of scientistic prejudice pervading the techno-logical age, then the implications, not least the ethical, are profound. Let's imagine then that I see an empty jug on the kitchen table the morning after a dinner party. Part of what makes it a jug, my ability to see the jug 'as' this jug involves its capacity to be 'empty'. Now the scientist will tell us that what we *actually* see is an object that isn't in fact 'empty' at all. They might tell us that what I see is an object composed of various materials, forming a cavity that is currently filled with a combination of (for the most part) nitrogen, oxygen, water vapour, argon, and carbon dioxide – 'the compound mixture of air'. But that is *not at all* what I 'see'. I 'see' instead a jug that is 'empty', the same jug – made from clay (earth) that was filled with wine last night (sky), wine (the divine gift formed of earth and sky) that we drank with our guests (mortals). It is the empty jug that will be filled with soapy water shortly, scrubbed clean, emptied, and left to dry on the draining board. It is the empty jug that will be filled with wine again the next time we entertain guests to celebrate, perhaps, some event or milestone in our lives (mortals). The jug reminds me of an empty jug that was used recently at my niece's Christening. The empty jug was immersed in a font and used to pour a little water over her head as part of a blessing (divinity). The scientist, Heidegger believes, will dismiss all of this claiming that we have "let ourselves be deceived by a semi-poetic manner of observation" when we invoke the emptiness of the jug (GA79: 8–9/8). And, the danger, for Heidegger, is that the current way that coming to presence/meaningfulness takes place is such that we are losing our very capacity to see things *as* 'things' any longer – and, we have to add, mortals as mortals. Everything is reduced to constant presence in quite an extreme and potentially irreversible way, a result that was already set in motion at the beginning of the history of Western metaphysics as we fell into oblivion as to what we mean when we say that things 'are', what the 'being' of things means. Heidegger is deeply alarmed at the extent and pace of the rampant and eliminative way everything is 'revealed' or rendered as 'real' for us in the

---

[36] See GA79: 8–9/8–9.

technological age. We are at the point that we may no longer be able to see things *as* things or humans as humans, as everything dissolves into a coherence of forces, resources, atoms, molecules, what have you:

> Within its purview, that of objects, the compelling knowledge of science has already annihilated the thing as thing long before the atomic bomb exploded. The explosion of the atomic bomb is only the crudest of all crude confirmations of an annihilation of things that occurred long ago: confirmation that the thing as thing remains nullified. (GA79: 8–9/8–9.)

The influence of the *Gestell* – technology's essential "enframing" or "imposition" – is so pervasive and consumptive as to have eliminated every other possibility of revealing and equalises and 'positions' everything under its levelling gaze. It threatens the very essence of the human being and our capacity to dwell historically in worlds.

The Fourfold

The reader will have noticed in the previous section that the jug (and the liquid it pours) have the terms *earth*, *sky*, *divinities*, and *mortals* in brackets after various instances of the use of the term [jug]. These four terms are collectively referred to as 'the fourfold' and come to occupy an important place in Heidegger's discussion of 'the thing'. The discussion of the fourfold has a direct impact on the ethical bond that Heidegger wants us to consider. However, we can only really begin to appreciate that impact once the meaning of the fourfold has been unpacked. In what follows then, we will try to explain why Heidegger discusses this ambiguous notion of the fourfold in the context of what he describes the 'thinging of the thing', that is, our experience of the thing *as* thing.

In the penultimate lecture in the Bremen series ("The Danger"), Heidegger describes 'world' as

> the still-concealed mirror-play of the fourfold of heaven and earth, mortals and divinities. To bring the world near is the thinging of the thing. Should the nearness that brings near be prohibited, then the thing as thing remains withheld.
>
> The universal requisitioning of positionality [*das Gestell*] allows all that presences to presence solely as **pieces of inventory of the standing reserve,** objects are no longer permitted, much less the thing as thing. (GA79: 46/44 Emphasis added)

Heidegger's language and imagery become notoriously abstruse as he continues to pursue his path of thinking in the decades following *Being and Time*. The issue of the fourfold has given rise to a good deal of abstract and complex discussions in the literature.[37] And yet, for all of that 'industry', the challenge remains to try and state as simply as possible what Heidegger might be driving at in the context of our discussion of the ethical exigencies of the technological age.[38]

Human beings are **mortal**; that is, we are the only creatures that are 'able' to die, that can be-towards-death. Recognising our finitude brings us before the nothing or nothingness; this in turn allows us to see how the nameless/the limitless/the abyssal (**divinities**) are the constant self-concealing backdrop to any instance of meaningful presence. This is the ineffable, inarticulable background to and future of any historical existence – the self-effacing, infinite correlate of all experience. To think god/divinity in an appropriate way is to think being and the nothing. There is a constant non-oppositional strife (i.e., a striving together) between that which refuses or resists presence and that which comes to presence for us. Our very ability to be is an ability also not to be, this is our utmost possibility, and each and every instance of significance in our lives is shaped by this possibility. We are a being-towards, we are futural, and we face the 'divine' understood as the nameless, the unfamiliar, the abyssal. This is the situation that we find ourselves in collectively. The **earth** is the dark, hidden 'stuff' from which our 'things' are made, and it is where our places are placed. It is the irreducible source of the material from which all of our 'things' are fashioned, but which will never itself be a thing and to which, in a way, all things return (Edwards, 2005: 461–462). The sky is stretched like a high, vaulted canopy over the earth. It lights up and darkens the earth where we reside. It nourishes the earth with rain and sun. It brings night, darkness, and wintry cold – withering. Night gives way to day, and vice versa. On the earth and underneath the sky the day can lengthen and shorten depending on the passing of the seasons and days according to our measure. The very measure echoes with reminders of how earth and sky are not reducible to our measure even as they are conditions for how we experience things meaningfully. Sky grants us the measure of time with our passing hours, days, months, seasons, and years, while also reminding us of the fact that this granting of measure will outstrip our

---

[37] For an extensive, book-length treatment of the notion of the fourfold, see Mitchell (2015).

[38] I am indebted to James C Edward's commendably lucid treatment of the fourfold here. A good deal of his analyses chime with what I am trying to argue for, even if his analyses are confined to simply trying to outline what Heidegger is concerned with in terms of *Gestell* and how the thinging of the thing and the fourfold take centre stage in Heidegger's thought. One slight criticism I would make is that there is a tendency to lapse into a quasi-existentialist reading, not least in terms of the account of death. There is no real mention then of the history of the metaphysics of presence, for example, or the relevance of what Heidegger has to say about being and nothingness and the notions of god or the divine in *that* context, not simply in terms of the nullifying or negation of our own existence but of the idea of the nameless in general. He mentions this in passing, but the account seems a little sparse as a consequence (see Edwards, 2005).

own time of measure. It points further to the possibility of what Edwards refers to as the numbing possibility of "pure, pointless time: time that is not history" (Edwards, 2005: 464), the time of meaninglessness and namelessness which is the ultimate possibility of all history, of all that is meaningful and named – a time, in effect, which is untimely.

This striving together of 'out-standing' human beings, facing the abyss, on the earth, underneath the sky is gathered in the unified appearance of thing as thing. And the way this unifying takes place in the thinging of thing emerges in the specific way the world worlds for us in any given era. That is, the appearance of things as things happens through a particular epoch-defining ordinance which governs the way everything appears or emerges meaningfully. This is what Heidegger refers to as "the worlding of the world". Again, the point here is that Heidegger is interested in meaningfulness, the experience of things *as* things. He is interested in the conditions or source of that meaningfulness and how it itself (the source – which is not to hypostasise 'it' or to treat it as a cause) is not a product of our own sense-making or subjectivity. Each occurrence of meaningful presence is a gathering of earth, sky, divinities, and mortals; and, as something shines forth as a thing, it carries the silent echo of the abyssal, the nothingness which is part of its possibilities (as opposed its actuality), which in turn points to the ultimate possibility of all meaningfulness, that is, meaninglessness.[39]

If we go back to the example of the jug – the potter makes the jug from clay (**earth**), we fill the jug with wine to share with friends on a summer's evening (**sky**), perhaps to mark something significant in our lives (**mortals**), and the event we celebrate or mark might be a birth, marriage, blessing, death or commemoration (**divinity**). The wine that we pour is the fruit of the vine that has ripened, been harvested, crushed, fermented, and bottled, that we have bought for an occasion or celebration, that is decanted into the jug, and that we now imbibe with friends following a toast or perhaps some commemorative words (**Earth, Sky, Mortals, Divinity**). The empty jug is lying ready to be filled with wine or water to be poured on some occasion or other. The pouring of the wine from the once empty and now refilled jug is a gathering and unifying of the fourfold in the appearance of the jug as jug. The emptiness involved is not properly understood as simply incapacity. As Heidegger explains, the 'scythe' and 'hammer' are not incapable of pouring wine or water in the same way that the empty jug is. In the act of pouring, we see the thinging of the thing, we see the jug as jug. The scientific description of the empty jug as a cavity filled with

---

[39] Heidegger signals as much in *Being and Time* in a particular statement concerning the ready-to-hand: "What oppresses us is not this or that, nor is it the summation of everything present-at-hand; it is rather the *possibility* of the ready-to-hand in general; that is to say, it is the world itself" (SZ: 187).

air does not capture any of this and it certainly does not render the notion of the empty jug obsolete.

If we draw the strands together here and understand the inter-relationship of world, being and the nothing, the truth (unconcealedness) of being, the fourfold, the thing as thing, and the history of how things emerge as things from one epoch to the next, we can hopefully begin to see how and why Heidegger's subsequent remarks concerning people murdered in the concentration camps are part of his more general concern with how we might discover our ethical obligations in the technological age. In the way that we take everything to 'be', the way everything is 'revealed' for us today, that is, through *Gestell*, we are blocked from 'nearness' to 'world' – "In the standing reserve [which is how everything is revealed/reduced through *Gestell*] objects are no longer permitted, much less the thing as thing" (GA79:45/44). Instead of seeing things as things, we see stockpiles of resources, composites of atoms, forces to be harnessed and controlled – and that extends, of course, to us mortals. Indeed, we have Human Resources departments anywhere that people work together (GA7: 18).

It's worth noting that Heidegger insists that while we are on the precipice in terms of falling ourselves into the standing reserve, in the original published essay at least, he nevertheless insists that *we* cannot ourselves merely become part of an inventory, simply reduced to resources. We remain the being through which this coming to presence of what is taken to be real at any given moment takes place, after all. This adds further weight to the claim that in the Bremen lectures (see the next subsection) Heidegger cannot be dismissing the claims to humanity of people in the death camps. In the same way that perishing cannot be attributed to the self-experience of the inmates and refers rather to the attitude of the perpetrators who have dehumanised people in the camps, seeing the same people as items of an inventory cannot be a description of the self-experience of the inmates. Rather, Heidegger is describing the attitude of the perpetrators who had dehumanised the people they murdered to the point that they were simply items in an inventory, and ultimately waste to be disposed of.

The Danger

Where we lose the capacity to see things *as* things "the refusal of world" takes place. The world still worlds "But the worlding of world is not ... properly experienced and correspondingly thought" (GA 79: 47/45). The way that we experience the real at any given moment has always and ever depended on the "still-concealed mirror-play of the fourfold" (GA 79: 47/45). It is this mirror-play of earth and sky, divinity and mortals which, in "the uniting whole of its presence ... guards everything that thingingly presences and absences between the four". In other words, we see what has emerged as thing and forget how the 'presence' of the thing involves the interplay of presence and absence within the historical world we are thrown into. World is what allows things to emerge *as* things; as a result of the worlding of the world, things emerge as meaningfully present. However, for the most part, our attention is drawn merely to the presence of what is currently present, while the worlding of the world conceals itself. We tend to overlook or forget the worlding of the world, it remains concealed from us.[40] The way that this worlding takes place has evolved from one epoch to the next culminating in the unique form of unconcealment taking place in the technological age, which, as noted earlier, Heidegger names *Gestell*. The happening of unconcealment, and thereby 'every way of being' (every kind of presencing), conceals itself, and this leads to forgetting or oblivion. This is what the so-called 'forgottenness of being' (*Seinsvergessenheit*) means at bottom: "that both the essence of being, presencing, and its essential provenance in Ἀλήθεια as the event of the essence of this, as well as Ἀλήθεια itself, all lapse into forgetfulness" (GA79: 48/50–51). As a result, this 'dynamic process' is unavailable to human perception and representation, which only appears to have access, in terms of direct perception and representation, to the actual, what is 'representable'. "For this reason, human thinking is unable to think the essence of unconcealment or the presencing in it . . . human thinking from the outset has forgotten the essence of being" (GA79: 48/50–51). The backdrop to this constant disclosure conceals itself, refuses itself. Part of how the real has revealed itself in successive epochs has been as constant presence; however, there is a dimension which has been forgotten since it conceals itself as each type of unconcealing takes place (as constant presence) and holds sway – to the point that this forgetting currently threatens to terminally block access to that other dimension. Heidegger now wants us to see how we are blocked from even having access to the thing *as* thing in the age of modern technology where *Gestell* governs the emergence of what appears as 'present' at any given moment. It is *das Gestell* that

> orders all that is present as what is constant of the **pieces of the inventory of the standing reserve**. In so ordering the standing reserve, positionality places all that is present into a state of distancelessness. Positionality concerns the presencing of all that presences as such. Positionality is thus in its essence the being of beings in its most extreme and presumably completed destiny. Positionality is the essence of modern technology. The essence of positionality is the being of beings itself, not everywhere and not from time immemorial, but rather now, here where the forgetting of the essence of being completes itself. (GA79: 51/48–49 Emphasis added)

---

[40] See GA79: 49/46–47.

This is the great danger that threatens us, and it is in this context that Heidegger sees the urgent need to revitalise ethics. Humanism and ethics, thought anew, are therefore very much at the heart of Heidegger's thinking. Heidegger sees our current situation as an emergency – we need to awaken genuine distress among human beings such that they recognise the devastation that is both on our doorstep and indeed has already taken place. It is in *this* specific context that Heidegger makes the following infamous remark about "the fabrication of corpses" in camps, which I accordingly cite in full.

> Are there times when we could have noticed *the* distress, the dominance of distresslessness? There are indications. Only we do not attend to them.
>
> Hundreds of thousands die in masses. Do they die? They perish. They are put down. Do they die? They become **pieces of inventory of a standing reserve** for the fabrication of corpses. Do they die? They are unobtrusively liquidated in annihilation camps. And even apart from such as these – millions now in China abjectly end in starvation. To die, however, means to carry out death in its essence. To be able to die means to be capable of carrying this out. We are only capable of it, however, when our essence is endeared to the essence of death. Indeed, in the midst of these innumerable dead, the essence of death remains disguised. Death is neither the empty nothing, nor is it merely the transition from one existence to another. *Death belongs in the Dasein of the human as appropriated from the essence of beyng.* (GA79: 55–56/ 53 Emphasis in bold added)

Further context for this passage is found in the analysis of death in *Being and Time* where Heidegger distinguishes between three different kinds of death: perishing (*Verenden*), demise (*Ableben*), and dying (*Sterben*) (SZ: 247). He is adamant that Dasein can never perish. The human being can 'demise' and the human being can 'die' in the sense of being-towards-death ('death' in the second sense then is dispositional, what Heidegger describes as 'a way to live'). However, perishing is a biological occurrence, and Dasein is not to be understood as a biological entity or a bio-anthropological thing for Heidegger.[41] Dasein is mortal, that is, we are 'able to die'. The moment we are no longer 'able to die', we are no longer Dasein, we are no longer a 'not yet', a being towards the future.

The background to and occasion for these remarks is also crucial here if we are to forestall wayward interpretations: Heidegger prepared these remarks for a series of public lectures on the topic of the essence of modern technology. This is often overlooked by commentators who loudly proclaim Heidegger's moral bankruptcy and accuse him of neutralising, minimising, or indeed denying the Holocaust. What further need do we have of interpretation? After all, you can read it for yourself; he compares Auschwitz to farming in

---

[41] For an extended discussion on this passage, see O'Brien (2022).

another passage![42] In other work, I have offered a series of extended reflections on this issue where I argue for a rather different, context-sensitive interpretation of this and other related passages. In my view it is clear, not least from the passages we have examined that prefigure these remarks, that Heidegger is condemning what has happened to people in the camps along with millions of other people who have died from famine in China. Heidegger warns that in the current destinal sending of meaningful presence, we no longer have any trace of the thing as thing – and are further guilty, at times, of not seeing mortals as mortals. The way everything is revealed now involves their dis-integration, reduction, and dis-solution into standing reserve. As he states again in the published essay on the essence of technology: when we no longer experience anything anymore as 'objects', when everything is 'object-less' standing reserve, we are in a perilous situation.

When considering earlier how we no longer experience even objects, only a standing reserve and stockpiles, and how everything is positioned and ordered for us so as to appear that way, Heidegger uses the term 'inventory'. We see things from the standpoint of their position in an inventory or as a resource to be disposed of as one sees fit. In the "Letter on Humanism" Heidegger urges, as noted earlier, that, in this predicament, that is, in the emergency that he associates with the age of modern technology, "the greatest care must be fostered on our ethical bond", as it accords with our essence as human beings. He is not, to be clear, making the category mistake of reducing genocide to agriculture (as is sometimes suggested – see footnote 42), rather he is highlighting the way everything emerges as meaningfully present in the age of *Gestell*. It is not that war, agriculture, and genocide are 'the same'. They share the same 'essence' – that is, they are coming to presence in the same way (i.e., through *Gestell*). That does not mean that Heidegger is claiming that there is no difference between tillage farming and the Holocaust. What he is drawing our attention to is the influence that *Gestell* exercises in every aspect of our lives. Granted, that does not alter the fact that he should have said something specific about the horrors of the Holocaust beyond this philosophical point. That is an undeniable failing. However, it is important to acknowledge that Heidegger *is* trying to think through these problems in a proto-ethical way.

Conversely, a number of critics read Heidegger here as arguing that some human beings are not fully Dasein (i.e., authentically human), that they didn't in fact 'die' in the camps because they are not properly human, and that this is the logical extension of some of his remarks in the 1930s.[43] However, even if one wanted to

---

[42] See GA79: 27/27. The passage in question is often misleadingly referred to as "the agriculture remark" by critics who denounce Heidegger for comparing the Holocaust to modern farming methods.

[43] See O'Brien (2022) for a detailed response to this kind of interpretation. Donatella di Cesare (2017), Emmanuel Faye (2012), and Bettina Bergo (2017) all offer variants of this interpretation.

take the view that it's *possible* to understand him this way, by way of response we can reproduce some of the ideas we examined earlier to the effect that we are all bound by our finitude to times and places and that this can and should be the basis for an originary ethics. As I have argued elsewhere,[44] I do not believe that Heidegger was extending his exclusionary vision of the 1930s to the specific remarks in Bremen and claiming that the Jewish people did not die because they were not really human beings to begin with. There is a way of construing things such that it can look like the remarks in Bremen, *taken out of context*, chime with some of his comments about the historylessness and worldlessness of various groups of people (including the Jewish people) in a series of lectures, texts, and notebooks from the 1930s. However, that simply doesn't strike me as a plausible reading of the passages here, where he is clearly warning us about the dangers of the technological age. He underlines the horrifying and distressing nature of these crimes against humanity, describing how mechanically and dispassionately these factories of death 'liquidated' human beings. 'Undying death' is a clear reference to the outlook of the perpetrators since human beings (understood as Dasein), for Heidegger, cannot perish in this way. The fact that Heidegger returns to the precise terminology of *Being and Time* is also telling, and he makes clear again within this series of lectures that while the animal can perish, the human being (understood as Dasein) can *never* perish. Hence, this is not, in my view, best understood as a reference to the self-experience of the victims. Furthermore, in the face of what he characterises as an emergency, Heidegger stresses the need to rethink ethics and humanism, to restore humanity by allowing us to see again the essence of what it is to be human. Heidegger sees all of this as distressing and horrifying, and as part of a planetary emergency that requires us to think carefully about how we are and should be ethically directed and bound. Even if one believes this to be entirely insufficient, it at least gives the lie to the idea that Heidegger is a Holocaust denier.

Granted, even if we accept the line of reasoning just elaborated, we might still have reservations. Why did Heidegger fail to *name*? Why not speak specifically about 'the Jews at Auschwitz', for example? Why ignore the shocking singularity of the Shoah? This is an extremely fraught and complicated issue. Given Heidegger's complicity as a member of the Nazi party; given that he was an avowed, vocal, and influential supporter of Nazi policy while rector of Freiburg University, and, given his gushing admiration for Hitler in the 1930s, many of his Jewish friends, students, and colleagues, quite reasonably, expected a word of contrition, an apology – at the very least, an unequivocal statement or admission. If Heidegger was going to venture anything at all in public, then this was the very least that one might have expected. Even if there are some compelling insights

---

[44] See O'Brien (2022).

concerning the horrors of the Holocaust in the Bremen lectures, we have to acknowledge that there is a failure on Heidegger's part as well. Heidegger might well be correct in seeing death camps as, in some ways, an expression of *Gestell*; but that is not enough! One can acknowledge the singularity of this wound in human history without treating it as ahistorical – to be singular does not mean to be beyond comprehension or history. This was an opportunity to state *unambiguously* how our ethical bond should specifically bar us from dehumanising whole swathes of people in this way and to *name* the places and the peoples he was alluding to. Heidegger could further have openly confessed his gross error in proclaiming repeatedly in the 1930s that Jewish people, even though historically bound like him through place, time, and language, were not his German 'siblings'.

That Heidegger was horrified by what had happened under the Nazi reign of terror is clear from his post-war correspondence with Jaspers. We find no trace of the apologetics or equivocations that befoul his correspondence with Marcuse here,[45] and it contains an important series of admissions in the context of assessing his remarks on the death camps in Bremen. Below are some telling excerpts from that correspondence:

> Since 1933, I no longer came to your house, not because a Jewish woman lived there, but because I **simply felt ashamed** ... When, at the end of the 1930s **the worst evil set in with vile persecutions**, I thought immediately about your wife. (Heidegger-Jaspers, 2003, 185: Emphasis added)
>
> **What I have reported can excuse nothing**; it can only explain to what extent and how far from year to year, as more viciousness came out, **the sense of shame also grew over having here and there, directly and indirectly, contributed to it**. (Heidegger-Jaspers, 2003: 189. Emphasis added)
>
> **Then came the persecution of the Jews, and everything fell into the abyss.** (Heidegger-Jaspers, 2003: 189. Emphasis Added)

3 Critics Corner

In recent decades, a number of scholars have bucked a trend alluded to in Section 1 and insisted that Heidegger *is* relevant in one way or another to ethics. Adopting a variety of interpretive approaches these scholars have been both critical of and receptive to what they take to be the ethical implications of Heidegger's thought.[46] In the prefatory material for Joanna Hodge's book on

---

[45] See Wolin (1993: 160–164).

[46] See for example Vogel (1994), Hodge (1995), Olafson (1998), Hatab (2000), Freeman (2010), Golob (2017). There have been other significant contributions, and no doubt some readers will be surprised at some omissions. Some readers may wonder as to why Lawrence Hatab's important book is not discussed in more detail. The reason, in short, is that Hatab spends more time looking

Heidegger and ethics we read that "Heidegger denied that his enquiries were concerned with ethics", whereas Hodge will set out to question "this self – understanding". Hodge introduces her project on the very first page with the following claim: "Heidegger himself writes very little about ethics, and then only to state that ethical questions are not his concern" (Hodge, 1). However, as we have seen above, that is something of an overstatement, or requires some qualification at least. Hodge proceeds to unfold a complex reading of a range of Heidegger's texts spanning the better part of his career going back as far as *Sein und Zeit*. Her primary objective is to retrieve the repressed ('bracketed', 'suspended') ethical dimension in Heidegger's thought, challenging what she sees as an excessively jaundiced view of metaphysics. Hodge does not concern herself with Heidegger's account of originary ethics to the same extent as we have in the foregoing. One way of characterising the difference in our approaches is to see Hodge as emphasising the shortcomings of Heidegger's approach where she is expanding on the hidden potential for ethical thinking in Heidegger. She offers a reading of Heidegger *beyond* Heidegger, rather than simply against Heidegger. Conversely, we have spent more time trying to make sense of Heidegger's explicit references to ethics.[47]

In a clear-sighted and often compelling entry on Heidegger and ethics for the *The Cambridge History of Moral Philosophy* (Golob and Timmerman, 2017), Sacha Golob offers a simple but robust critique of what he takes to be Heidegger's ethical thinking. According to Golob, given the indeterminate, second-order nature of Heidegger's account of authenticity, which Golob also reads as issuing an ethical imperative, Heidegger's account, while *appearing* to have some kind of normative bite, could effectively be used to condone any kind of practical activity (he uses the rather diabolical example of a torturer) as consistent with the successful attainment of authenticity. Formulated in this way, that would appear to be an unfortunate implication of Heidegger's account of authenticity.

There are a number of ways one might try to respond on Heidegger's behalf here, even if Golob raises important and difficult questions for Heidegger. First, it's not clear that Heidegger needs to concede that the notion of authenticity is straightforwardly prescriptive in this way. Heidegger is looking to show that the real backdrop to meaningfulness and significance needs to be radically overhauled and that we do not in fact have the constancy of metaphysical principles to prop up our understanding of things. In that sense, as Golob correctly points

---

at ways to rethink Heidegger's philosophy in the context of existing moral philosophy and not as much time unpacking Heidegger's attempts to offer an originary ethics.

[47] Hodge does begin to make some headway on some of our own key concerns in the concluding chapter of the book, foregrounding, for example, the relevance of *Fürsorge*, care, the self, and others.

out, Heidegger believes that our meaning-making occurs ultimately against the backdrop of meaninglessness and indeterminacy (nothingness). However, it is important to note here that Heidegger does not offer an existentialist response to this situation, since we *do* in fact retain the capacity to live in meaningfully rich historical worlds nonetheless.

Think again of Nietzsche's madman: if one is to succumb to despair and assume that unless the traditional mainstays of moral understanding (and metaphysics more generally) are in place that we henceforth will be plunged into darkness and amorality, then one is missing the point of Nietzsche's parable. We may not be able to rely on the metaphysical principles dreamt up by the likes of Kant, but the challenge is to see clearly how we live and understand all the same. Once we get straight on the historicity of our situation and our radical finitude, we need to rethink ethics outside of the illusions of the Kantian dream of placing ethics on a footing impregnable to the vicissitudes of human preference or situatedness. That is not to succumb to despair or evaluative nihilism. Instead, we are obliged to think very carefully about the nature of our ethical intuitions and obligations. A recurring tendency among critics of relativism, for instance, is to assume that the only way that we can avoid evaluative nihilism is to insist on ethical absolutism. This is surprising for a number of reasons, not the least of which being the fact that it refuses to consider the possibility that various other non-absolutist theories might hold some weight. It is problematic in at least two other ways as well. First, it's question begging. And second, it is very often an argument from desire (e.g., that we couldn't possibly want to live in a world lacking the security of absolute principles) rather than an argument based on facts or to the best explanation.

Second (in response, again, to Golob's critique), one could argue that it is a little unfair to criticise the notion of authenticity for being normatively undercooked when it is clearly not meant to demonstrate what the 'specifics' for living an authentic life might involve. True, it is a preparatory kind of thinking. However, the fact that it is prior to a practical ethics is hardly grounds for attacking it for not offering a practical ethics. As a third and final response, one might contest the implication that Heidegger doesn't have the resources to even begin to think ethically. In this connection one could point to the primacy of being-with and notions such as *Fürsorge* (specifically, in the mode of leaping-ahead). There is also certainly scope to consider whether certain attitudes or actions are consistent with viewing another human being in accord with their essence as human beings. Granted, this may not offer us a series of concrete practical rules; but neither does it mean that these discussions offer no food for thought in terms of how we might engage with others. The controversial remarks in Bremen (discussed above) certainly seem to suggest that to treat others in certain ways is inhumane, ways that are not in keeping with their essence as human beings, a catastrophic failure to see or treat them as Dasein (i.e., to fail to leap ahead of them as thrown beings-towards-death in their own right). Thus, Heidegger may not have to concede that one can be an authentic human being while treating others in an abhorrent way – torturing them, for instance. He could argue that this is to *not* see them 'essentially' as human beings. Granted, and I take this to be something Golob is keenly aware of, we do have to be careful in terms of how far we canvass on Heidegger's behalf here. After all, Heidegger was clearly frustrated at the tendency to read *Being and Time* as a kind of transcendentally ideal, Kantian work, or a work of idealism, or subjectivism, when his goal was to overcome idealism and metaphysics and to show how nothingness, meaninglessness, and sheer contingency (as discovered through our own finitude) pervade our historical worlds. Indeed, his attempts to express this thought, as he himself acknowledges, struggle in the 'nets of language'. In trying to show how Heidegger can help us to determine what is inhumane and to censure actions that fail that 'measure' of our humanity, we must therefore be careful not to formulate something beyond what Heidegger himself offers. Heidegger is concerned with what we might call the 'source'[48] of how things matter to us, what it means to be human, and how things should and do become meaningful and significant to us. This in turn can inform our understanding of how we can feel bound in various ways. Nevertheless, it is important to remember that Heidegger has no desire to formulate a transcendental or universal principle on that basis – that is, a substantive, ahistorical, transcendental principle to guide our actions. This leads Golob to conclude with a timely and salutary warning. When a philosopher's work is understood to have profound implications for humanity but remains at such a preparatory level when it comes to the concrete questions of what it is to live a good life – there are pitfalls. It is certainly more amenable to distortion and can be moulded more easily (if entirely inappropriately) to fit even the most noxious of outlooks and political programs. We see this happening with alarming frequency today, where Heidegger's thought is appropriated by extreme right-wing populists and intellectuals. Heidegger himself betrayed the nuts and bolts of his own thought at times in his antisemitic, right-wing, conservative enthusiasm for the Nazi party.[49] As I have argued elsewhere, while Heidegger might well manage to highlight the radical indeterminacy and nothingness against which all meaningfulness occurs, he nevertheless relies on what are also clearly shared features of human existence as part of that

---

[48] It's important not to make the mistake of thinking 'source' causally here. That repeats the mistake made in thinking of God as first cause.

[49] See O'Brien (2015, 2022).

account. Those same features of our profoundly historical identity are in fact what undermine his own attempts to justify an exclusionary politics from within the constraints of his own thought.

In *Heidegger and the Ground of Ethics: A Study of Mitsein*, Frederick Olafson zeros in on Heidegger's account of *Mitsein* (being-with) in *Being and Time* with a view to extracting an ethics which, Olafson argues, Heidegger himself fails to produce. Olafson further insists that Heidegger fails to explain "how we can be authentic together". And yet, in his analysis of *Mitsein*, Olafson acknowledges that Heidegger offers some important insights and observations. It is not just "an empirical fact", for example, that there are other people; rather, "our being with" other people that are 'like' ourselves is "a constitutive element in our own mode of being as it is in theirs". Moreover, this is something that we cannot do justice to "as long as we approach it via traditional philosophical routes like the theory of empathy". Olafson goes on to argue that Heidegger invokes another notion that has an "unmistakably ethical character", namely, *Fürsorge*. He describes *Fürsorge* as

> one human being's caring about another – and it is this caring that he declares to be, in its several modalities, central to our being with one another. On the strength of these theses, he is even willing to go so far as to state that we are, as he puts it, 'for the sake of others' (*umwillen Anderer*). Because this idea was never developed further and Heidegger's occasional reflections on ethics in his later period take quite a different line, we have no explanation of how the concept of *Mitsein* generates the notion of *Fürsorge*. Significantly, however, he claims that 'resoluteness' – an existential virtue closely akin to authenticity – 'pushes us into a caring *Mitsein* with others'. (Olafson, 1998: 3–4)

Olafson's overview here already forewarns the reader of significant interpretive shortcomings that are likely to mar his analysis. For one thing, Olafson appears to have ignored the notion of collective authenticity as that might be developed on the basis of §74 of *Being and Time*.[50] Second, a brief analysis of the notion of leaping-ahead would already have helped to clarify Heidegger's reasons for stating that resoluteness 'pushes us into a caring *Mitsein* with others'. To see another person as thrown towards death or as a being-towards-death in their own right allows us to make sense of what Olafson appears to see as an enigmatic and under-developed claim on Heidegger's part.

It is also surprising that in a long footnote on Heidegger's "Letter on Humanism" Olafson makes no mention of (and thus appears to have overlooked) the significance of Heidegger's extended discussion of the importance

---

[50] Apart from a fleeting reference towards the end of the text, there is no real attempt to consider this, beyond alluding to its shortcomings (as Olafson sees it). See Olafson (1998: 91).

of the ethical bond for human beings in the technological age. Instead, he recycles the view that Heidegger's later work is inconsistent with *Being and Time* (the discontinuity thesis), is profoundly anti-humanist, and rejects the very possibility that ethics might in any way be relevant to his thinking. As we have seen in the foregoing, this caricature of Heidegger is deeply misleading and is undermined within the very text that Olafson adduces as support for this interpretation. Finally, given the book's focus, the frequent use of terms such as 'alter' and 'ego', along with a brief attempt to situate Heidegger in a certain existential phenomenological context with the likes of Sartre, one would expect a discussion of or, at the very least, some mention of Levinas. Moreover, given that Levinas criticises Heidegger's account in *Being and Time* for failing to do justice to the ethical relation to the other that precedes all else, it is certainly surprising then that Levinas' name never appears in the text.[51]

In *The Fragile We: Ethical Implications of Heidegger's 'Being and Time'*, Lawrence Vogel emphasises what he sees as the "universalistic implications of ... authentic Being-with-Others".[52] His approach, his critiques of some of the orthodox interpretations of Heidegger's account of authenticity, and his account of the possible ethical implications of that account intersect with our own in a number of ways, even if we diverge on some crucial interpretive issues. One of the major differences between our interpretation and Vogel's concerns the correct way to read Heidegger's critique of conventional morality in *Being and Time* and elsewhere. Vogel takes it as a given that Heidegger rejects the very idea of morality/ethics tout court when, if we pay closer attention, what Heidegger actually rejects are conventional forms of morality. However, that is not to foreclose the very idea of what Heidegger refers to in "Letter on Humanism" as the 'ethical bond'. What Heidegger is interested in rather is how we might approach the question of ethics having realised the futility of an approach based on a problematic metaphysics.

---

[51] No doubt some readers will arch an eyebrow at this criticism of Olafson given the decision not to engage with Levinas' critique of Heidegger in this Element. The reason for this omission is that (as we have seen in the foregoing) it's not clear, contra Levinas, that Heidegger replaces ethics with ontology. Having said as much, Heidegger's own account of being-with-others, relationality, and the social can seem rather thin and anaemic at times (not least in *Being and Time*). Levinas wants to offer more in terms of the irreducibility of the other to oneself, the need to avoid the tendency to assimilate the other to oneself, what have you. Notwithstanding, Levinas does not really engage with Heidegger's later attempts to articulate an originary ethics. And, given the space constraints of such a short text, we do not have the scope to pursue some of Levinas' more *Being and Time* specific criticisms. For an interesting discussion of Levinas's critique of Heidegger that expands on some relevant concerns see Thomson (2009).

[52] Irene McMullin offers an interesting reconstruction of Heidegger's account of being-with, which she characterises as Heideggerian intersubjectivity. See McMullin (2013)

Vogel argues that Heidegger's account of authentic Dasein appears to over-emphasise the individual, isolated nature of Dasein at times. In some other work, I have also examined a number of problematic passages which appear to be incompatible with Heidegger's insistence on the relational nature of Dasein, but which do anticipate his attempts to defend an exclusionary conception of a German Dasein of the people in the 1930s.[53] Nevertheless, these erroneous moves by Heidegger, in the main, fly in the face of the overwhelmingly relational nature of his account and don't really tally with the most plausible and uncomplicated readings of the accounts of Dasein, authenticity, and being-towards-death. Vogel argues that

> regard for the other's potential for authenticity … is essential to respect for the other as a person … Insofar as the authentic individual understands himself as transcending the past … others are revealed to him as 'fellow transcendences' … thrown into the same world as he is, yet transcending it just as he does. (Vogel, 88)

He goes on to invoke Caputo's reading in this regard:

> insofar as authenticity requires owning up to our shortcomings – affirming the limitations and frailties that come with finitude – one should be moved by *compassion* for others who are 'siblings of the same flux, brothers and sisters in the same dark night' … the solitude into which I am cast when I face my mortality and my responsibility for making something of my own life is precisely what makes possible the insight that 'we are a community of mortals bound together by our common fears and lack of metaphysical grounds.' (Vogel, 97)

Vogel manages to weave together a variety of interpretations along with his own which results in a compelling account of what authentic relating to others might look like, and how it is relevant to our ethical consideration of others. I would argue that Vogel is effectively reconstructing the best available interpretation of Heidegger's account in *Being and Time*, and the only one that really makes sense given the theoretical framework and implications of that account. However, he insists that Heidegger himself fails to follow through on those same implications; indeed, he asks: "But then why doesn't Heidegger say this? (Vogel, 100)".

There are a number of ways that one can respond here. (1) Vogel appears to have succumbed to a common failing of interpreters of the account of authenticity in *Being and Time*. That is, he ignores Heidegger's constant reminders that his goal is to try to answer the question concerning the meaning of being. The account of authenticity is a step along the way towards answering that question.

---

[53] See O'Brien (2015, 2022) for extensive discussions of these issues.

He requires some phenomenological testimony to support his belief that nothingness and absence play a significant role in our own experience and that there is a hidden backdrop to disclosure which is a part of how anything emerges as meaningfully present – that this is part of how we experience ourselves and (ideally) others. However, examining the moral implications of these phenomenological discoveries is not the immediate goal of *Being and Time*. Hence, the desire for something like a chapter or section on the ethics of authenticity in *Being and Time* is always going to be frustrated. But the lack of such a section is not tantamount to vetoing the very *possibility* of an ethics, one that is clearly consistent with the theoretical requirements of the early account of authenticity, and yet, one that does not tally with the exclusionary posture Heidegger adopted in the 1930s.

(2) Heidegger does indeed appear to equivocate at times on the relationality of Dasein, and appears to valorise the isolated, individual, non-relationality of authentic Dasein (a non-relational identity later re-conceived as the authentic German Dasein of a people). However, as Vogel himself points out, these are neither necessary nor even logically coherent implications of Heidegger's account. The shortcomings of what Vogel describes as the 'existentialist' and the 'historicist' readings of the account of authenticity are such that they ignore the scope of Heidegger's account of authentic Dasein, a scope he often struggled with, but one which he was never, ultimately, able to suppress (successfully at least).[54] It is the same scope to the account of being-towards-death that he reaffirms in his Bremen lectures to condemn the treatment of inmates in death camps during the Holocaust. Vogel's interpretation, "which draws out the latent universalistic implications of Heidegger's account of authentic Being-with-Others" (Vogel, 105) is what he calls the 'cosmopolitan' reading. He further claims that this cosmopolitan reading "answers the charge of moral nihilism to which fundamental ontology is vulnerable when it is interpreted along either existentialist or historicist lines" (Vogel, 105). While Heidegger would clearly

---

[54] In chapters two and three of *The Fragile We*, Vogel unpacks what he refers to as the 'existentialist' and 'historicist' interpretations of Heidegger's account of authenticity respectively. Vogel sees Sartre, Rorty and Olafson as prominent exponents of the 'existentialist' interpretation. The existentialist reading suggests that the human being is a 'radical chooser' – "floating unhinged above value-free facticity (Vogel, 47)". The 'historicist' interpreters of *Being and Time* (including Guignon and Fackenheim) insist that human beings "can never rise above the particular time and place into which one has been cast: the heritage and community to which one already belongs". The isolated, radical subject of existentialism, according to the historicist reading, "is an abstraction because freedom arises as the reappropriation of a social context of meaning in which one already participates (Vogel, 50)". The problem with the historicist reading, for Vogel, is that it runs the risk of simply transferring the isolated, atomistic outlook of the radical chooser onto the isolated community and "does not account for how we move and mediate among different contexts, heritages, communities" (Vogel, 69).

recoil from the appellation 'cosmopolitan', the thrust of the argument is attract-ive. Once Heidegger's account is reconstructed in this way, according to Vogel, it is shored up against the charges it remains susceptible to under the existen-tialist or historicist readings. However, Vogel suggests that his 'cosmopolitan' reading of authentic being-with-others requires that "Heidegger be read *against* Heidegger" (Vogel, 105). And, while Heidegger certainly bridled against cosmopolitanism with a rather unsavoury provincialist attitude at times, that does not in fact stem from any theoretical necessity in *Being and Time*. Granted, Heidegger certainly betrayed the theoretical underpinnings of his own account of Dasein and authenticity in *Being and Time* during the 1930s in a range of seminars, lectures, notebooks, and speeches. However, that is not to say that the account of authentic being-with-others that Vogel favours requires a violent reinterpretation of *Being and Time*. Instead, it is simply drawing out the neces-sary implications of the most plausible interpretation of the account of authentic Dasein and its co-existence with others.

The Kantian aspiration that Vogel frequently tries to smuggle into his recon-struction is one that Heidegger would likely challenge as inauthentic since it requires us to reason from an ahistorical and anonymous standpoint. It is a discharging of personal responsibility in the face of situations where we do not have the comfort of metaphysical constants (a metaphysics of morals, if you like). Heidegger offers us a starting point for how we should think, namely, in accord with our essence as human beings. That would hardly entail, however, that we are obliged to tell the truth no matter the circumstance, including, for example, the dire situation of being pressed by an axe murderer for the location of another human being when we suspect that the axe-toting individual in question might well be bent on visiting grievous harm on the same poor soul. We can acknowledge how we are bound as thrown, situated beings, but that does not prevent us from taking ownership of the challenges we face in these situations. To the contrary, part of what moves us to act and/or to take responsi-bility is the fact that we recognise the commitments or obligations we feel as people from a time and place. This same situatedness further leaves room for our ability to deliberate not as ahistorical, rationalist automatons, but as situated, historical people who can exercise our judgement.[55] How these obligations and duties develop as our gaze moves outward to wider arcs of concern is not something to be determined rigidly. Instead, we rely on our common humanity and respect for our essence as ek-sistent human beings to

---

[55] We don't have the space to engage with the debate between moral particularism and generalism here. In an interesting (if speculative) attempt to expand on Heidegger's brief remarks on 'metontology' in a 1929 lecture course, Lauren Freeman looks to sketch a Heideggerian ethics, which she characterises as a 'moderate particularism'. See Freeman (2010).

promote dialogue among people from different cultures and traditions. We do not look to eradicate specificity or difference; rather, we look to increase recognition and inclusion. That is not to lobby for an absolute principle of toleration, as the moral realist would charge, rather, the challenge is to think differently.

Vogel simply goes wrong when he keeps insisting that a weakness of Heidegger is his refusal to countenance any possibility of ethical implications arising from his project in *Being and Time*. Heidegger's remarks on ethics in "Letter on Humanism" clearly disqualify this interpretation. Towards the end of his book, Vogel tries to reinforce this point arguing that morality can only ever be "an inauthentic mode of existence". What Heidegger makes very clear in his "Letter on Humanism" is that he is against a certain kind of superficial morality. That is not to say that his attempt to overcome the metaphysics of presence and pay attention to the essence of the human being has no ethical implications. He could hardly have been more explicit about this in "Letter on Humanism". Despite these criticisms, our own interpretation of 'Letter on Humanism' clearly intersects with certain aspects of Vogel's 'cosmopolitan' reading, as he draws out the implications of Heidegger's accounts of Dasein, authenticity, being-with, and being-towards-death (notwithstanding Heidegger's lack of fidelity to those implications in a range of texts in the 1930s). As Vogel rightly concludes:

> My awareness of the groundlessness of my own Being-in-the-world is not the basis of existentialist anarchism or historicist relativism. Rather, it provides an experiential basis for the central requirement of a cosmopolitan or universalistic morality: respect for all persons as equal members of 'the family of humankind.'
>
> And beyond providing the basis for an *obligation* to respect the dignity of others, it can be contended that an authentic relation to one's own fragile finitude allows one to feel *compassion* for others who are acknowledged as 'brothers and sisters in the same dark night.' Owning up to one's own mortality, on this reading, awakens one from the sleep of indifference to the existence of others that characterize everyday life first of all and most of the time. (Vogel, 106)

Again, we detect an attempt to weave a Kantian imperative into this interpretation of Heidegger which seems ill-fitting. Nonetheless, the crucial thing to note is that whatever it may be to be morally responsible or to establish an 'ethical bond', it will be and *must* be grounded in our essence as human beings, which is, effectively, what Vogel contends. Vogel manages to draw out the obvious implications of Heidegger's account through his 'cosmopolitan' interpretation and he correctly identifies where the 'historicist' approach often goes awry.

Nevertheless, we do still have to acknowledge that Heidegger is in something of a bind here. The historicist interpretation remains key to Heidegger, and he simply would not disavow it completely. This is where he runs into problems, of course, since he can hardly deny that other people from other times and places end up as members of their communities in similar ways. The challenge is to see how the local acts as portal to the universal but without having to forfeit our sense of the local as being important and integral to us. It is never something to be bypassed or suppressed.[56] Unless we are to distort Heidegger's thinking in ways that go too far, we need an account that acknowledges how Heidegger might try to preserve the historicist approach while allowing for the fact that there is a wider backdrop to that historicism that he cannot evade and, indeed, at times actively embraces.

Authenticity and Ethics

Describing authenticity in Heidegger as a non-normative notion may seem rather perverse and/or confusing. Nevertheless, in *Being and Time*, it is clear, for example, that our lives are, even when lived authentically, a mixture of authenticity and inauthenticity. To live authentically is to live a life among other people, with their various social roles and functions, while also understanding the disclosive role of our temporality. Thus, the authentic life is a mixture of authentic and inauthentic modes of existence. However, that is not to say that Heidegger does not have concerns about what kind of inauthentic life we may be forced to live due to the way the history of the metaphysics of presence has culminated in the age of technology. It is certainly true that a life lived exclusively in the mode of inauthenticity and publicness, not least in the technological age, would fail to live up to the requirements of authenticity for Heidegger. It is further true that this kind of inauthenticity is described in what can sound like moralistic terms at times.

Nevertheless, it is important to remember that an inauthentic life would *not* necessarily be 'immoral' (in the conventional sense) or 'dissolute'. One could be living a perfectly 'moral' life and be entirely inauthentic. Indeed, even those who hold themselves to the strictest applications of absolute, universal principles, who refuse to succumb to the demands of the crowd, behaving entirely as non-conformists when faced with moral obligations, may well, themselves, be acting or living inauthentically. Heidegger believes that morality, ordinarily construed, is itself an entirely inauthentic notion. It is either something embraced as a 'norm' by *das Man* or it is something that anyone/everyone *should* do, regardless of one's

---

[56] See Joyce's remarks to Power in the epigraph to the introduction.

particular situation, and is thus a forsaking of the demands of personal responsibility in favour of an abstract universal principle.

Morality, in both senses, is an entirely anonymous enterprise, it is *not one's 'own'* response to a situation and, therefore, cannot be authentic (*'eigentlich'*, with the stress on *'eigen'* here). Instead, one acts or is directed by what 'anyone' should do at any time; that is, one acts according to what one thinks 'everyone' should do or according to what one thinks everyone else already thinks one should do. To challenge this approach to ethical reasoning is not to valorise voluntarism or egocentrism or to suggest that we have no way to proceed. Rather, we need to get clear on how we should think ethically and in ways that involve authentically responding to situations and understanding the proper ground and nature of the claims that a genuine ethical bond can place on us. Ethics in the sense that Heidegger wants to think about it is operating at a level prior to conventional normativity.

Existentialist Interpretations of Authenticity

Commentators who read Heidegger's account of authenticity and being-towards-death through the lens of what they take to be orthodox existentialism are guilty of a common mistake. Vogel discusses this in some detail under the umbrella of what he sees as existentialist misreadings of Heidegger's account of authenticity and the discussion of being-towards-death in particular. The mistake made is to assume that once the idea of abstract, universal moral principles or ideals is discredited, that there is nothing left to generate ethical commitments apart from extreme subjectivity. We are radically free and can 'justify' any kind of behaviour whatsoever. Anything and everything 'is', quite literally, 'permissible'.

Leaving to one side the question as to whether all existentialists would accept this caricature of their position, one thing that Vogel and I agree on is that this cannot be the kind of view that Heidegger would espouse. For one thing, the notions of freedom and autonomy involved are simply irreconcilable with anything we find in Heidegger. Indeed, this is clearly part of why Heidegger rejects the appellation [existentialism] as appropriate to his thinking. If we think again of Nietzsche's account of the Madman in *The Gay Science*, we might be able to clarify where things go wrong here. Nietzsche is not himself 'the Madman'; the Madman is rather more like the clichéd existentialist caricature that everyone is familiar with, reeling from what he takes to be the Black Hole left by the death of God and the inevitable consequence that everything must now be permissible. For Nietzsche, the Madman has been disabused of an illusion, and he is experiencing extreme disillusion at the sudden realisation that the eternal, universal principles of metaphysics and morals have been discredited. He cannot see anything but chaos and devastation as a result. However, to embrace absurdity, or to resign oneself to moral nihilism (or any other kind of nihilism) as a consequence is unwarranted. What both Nietzsche and Heidegger are exploring is the nature of the challenge faced. In Heidegger's case, he is asking how we can secure some sense or meaning for both humanism and 'the ethical bond', not in terms of metaphysical constants, but in accord with our human essence.

Cosmopolitanism versus Provincialism

We live in an era where the term 'cosmopolitan' is, for many, a byword for inclusivity and tolerance. For those of us with liberal and/or left-leaning sensibilities, we can scarcely imagine it as anything other than an outlook to be commended and indeed recommended. Now, I do not for one moment want to suggest that the cruder and more bigoted elements of Heidegger's anti-cosmopolitan provincialism are justifiable or anything other than offensive. However, it is worth remembering that the idea of a global citizen or citizen of the world was looked on with considerable suspicion and often resisted by those witnessing the increasing pace of globalisation in the twentieth century. On the fiftieth anniversary of the Easter 1916 rising, for example, the then Irish President Eamon de Valera warned people against an 'amorphous cosmopolitanism':

> In the realization of all this our national language has a vital role. Language is a chief characteristic of nationhood – the embodiment, as it were, of the nation's personality and the closest bond between its people. No nation with a language of its own would willingly abandon it. The peoples of Denmark, Holland, Norway, for example, learn and know well one or more other languages, as we should, of course, for the sake of world communication, commerce and for cultural purposes; but they would never abandon their native language, the language of their ancestors, the language which enshrines all the memories of their past. They know that without it they would sink into an amorphous cosmopolitanism – without a past or a distinguishable future. (de Valera, 2006: 139)[57]

De Valera was a staunch nationalist, having been a prominent member of Ireland's armed resistance to British rule before embarking on a political career in the new Republic where he had roles as Taoiseach (prime minister) and later president of the Republic of Ireland. It's worth noting that 1966 was the year of

---

[57] Eamon de Valera. "These were all good men". Speech on the fiftieth anniversary of the Easter Rising, 10 April 1966. Montefiore (2006: 139).

Heidegger's infamous interview with *Der Spiegel*. Are de Valera's remarks as problematic as Heidegger's exhortations to the German people at various junctures? Are they on some kind of continuum? Or are they different in *kind*? Obviously, we don't hear anything as repugnant as the antisemitism and ethnic chauvinism we find in Heidegger's private notebooks or indeed some of the speeches and seminars from the 1930s. Nevertheless, is there still a certain continuity here? Is there necessarily a kind of exclusionary vision involved? Or are we simply dealing with sentiments that are, while perhaps jarring to those of us with the more liberal and inclusive sensitivities we associate with left-leaning or even centrist political outlooks today, not inherently problematic? Perhaps the balance to be struck involves an acknowledgement of our historical and cultural specificity that allows for the possibility of intercultural dialogue and integration.[58]

What then are we to make of the hugely problematic nature of Heidegger's attempts to put some of his thinking concerning Dasein, authenticity and the notion of an authentic Dasein of a people in the service of an abhorrent political vision? Heidegger's entrenched adherence to a Germanophilic provincialism is very disturbing at times. He tries to deflect with revisionist retrospectives in texts such as "Letter on Humanism". Nevertheless, his thinking clearly suffered from a certain shortcoming or blindspot (for a period of time, at the very least) in that he failed (or refused) to discern how his rigid adherence to an exclusionary provincialism was simply incompatible with the philosophical ideas he looked to connect it to. After all, human beings *in general* are thrown, historical beings whose worlds are run through by the constant interplay of presence and absence. This is already clear in *Being and Time*, even if he tries to renege on the theoretical necessity of this very thought at times.

We find an instance of Heidegger's revisionism in this context in "Letter on Humanism" where he adds some nuance and qualifies his comments on Germans and the German language and insists that he is not advocating nationalism or jingoism. This is very obviously a retreat from the rather more militant and exclusionary stance he took before the war, when he insisted that the German people needed to first be on their own and non-relational, before then looking outwards to be with other nations. His qualifying of these views in some later texts appears to be far more permissive. In other words, he examines our existence as members of historical communities, conditioned by our time, place, and language, while allowing for our capacity to see other communities as 'like' us and as 'humanised' in similar ways:

---

[58] It's not entirely clear that this is quite what de Valera had in mind.

> The clearing grants nearness to being. In this nearness, in the clearing of the *Da*, the human being dwells as the ek-sisting one without yet being able properly to experience and take over this dwelling today. In the lecture on Hoelderlin's elegy 'Homecoming' (1943) this nearness 'of' being, which the *Da* of Dasein is, is thought on the basis of *Being and Time*; it is perceived as spoken from the minstrel's poem; from the experience of the oblivion of being it is called the 'homeland.' The word is thought here in an essential sense, not patriotically or nationalistically, but in terms of the history of being. The essence of the homeland, however, is also mentioned with the intention of thinking the homelessness of contemporary human beings from the essence of being's history . . . 'German' is not spoken to the world so that the world might be reformed through the German essence; rather, it is spoken to the Germans so that from a destinal belongingness to other peoples they might become world-historical along with them. (GA 9: 168–169/257)[59]

This more nuanced and qualified approach is clearly an attempt to revise and/or sanitise the more extreme views that he had peddled in the 1930s. It is impossible to read this passage from the late 1940s and not recall Heidegger's appeal to the German people to support Hitler's 1933 plebiscite:

> It is not ambition, not desire for glory, not blind obstinacy, and not hunger for power that demands from the Führer that Germany withdraw from the League of Nations. It is only the clear will to unconditional self-responsibility in enduring and mastering the fate of our people. This is *not* a turning away from the community of nations. On the contrary – with this step, our people is submitting to that essential law of human existence to which every people must first give allegiance if it is still to be a people. It is only out of the parallel observance by all peoples of this unconditional demand of self-responsibility that there emerges the possibility of taking one another seriously so that a community can be confirmed.[60] (Heidegger, 1993: 48)

---

[59] We cannot simply ignore the fact that what Heidegger appeared to be saying quite explicitly for a period of time was *precisely* that the world 'needed' to be 'reformed through the German essence'. Heidegger certainly seems to equivocate on this issue. I am grateful to Daniel Dahlstrom for flagging some interesting discussions in a number of Heidegger's lectures on Hölderlin, including the Hölderlin-inspired idea of the necessity of the alien and the concomitant need to reach out to them. In his own *Heidegger Dictionary*, 2nd ed., pp. 303f we find the following relevant summary: "Its [Hölderlin's poetry's] retrieval of the originary also exemplifies the unique law of Hölderlin's work and the basic law of history as fate: Coming into one's own only via 'the sojourn in the foreign' (52: 175). It is necessary not merely to commemorate and thus preserve the foreign in order to appropriate what is one's own but to think the place from which 'what is coming must first be said and back to which the having been must be sheltered, so that this foreigner itself can be its own' (4: 150). As this last remark suggests, what is essential is how the foreign is to be engaged: unselfishly, wholeheartedly, in a greeting (4: 96; 52: 51ff; see GA 52)". These again are further examples of Heidegger considering a more nuanced and inclusive approach to the issues of homeland and the foreign.

[60] Martin Heidegger. "German Men and Women" (10 November 1933). Quoted in Richard Wolin (1993: 48).

Heidegger makes similar remarks at a rally in support of Hitler the following day. Leaving to one side our revulsion at the fact that Heidegger acts as apologist for Hitler's dictatorial designs and ignores the naked menace already obvious in his foreign policy, we are forced again to consider the obscene attempts to put his own thinking in the service of Nazism. This is related to Heidegger's attempts to articulate something like an authentic Dasein of a people in a number of places, which in turn is an extrapolation from authentic Dasein to something like Dasein 'writ large' as a community or 'people'.

In *Being and Time*, conversely, Heidegger had gone to considerable lengths to underline the fundamental relationality of Dasein. This relationality is a feature of our identity and constitution that we cannot get behind. There is no prior state that Dasein occupies before its relational identity.[61] However, there are times where Heidegger appears to equivocate on this crucial insight.[62] He repeats these equivocations (having moved now to the notion of an authentic Dasein of a people) in some of his speeches and texts from the 1930s, in order to bolster his political views and to establish continuity between his philosophical views and his valorisation of the German people. As we can see in the passage from "Letter on Humanism" above, there is a definite softening of the earlier more extreme outlook in favour of a much more nuanced understanding of what it might be to be a German person in this context. Heidegger makes a similarly qualified claim in one of the Bremen lectures:

> The internationality of scientific language is the starkest proof of its uproot-edness from the soil and lack of homeland, though this by no means says that rootedness in the soil and what is homely of language would be in the least bit guaranteed, determined, or even founded by what is merely national. What is homely in a high language thrives only in the region of the uncanny claim of an essential stillness in the essence of beyng. (GA79: 65–66/62)

This is an attempt to bring his thinking back in line with his views on the essence of the human being and the concomitant idea of an authentic community, but without the chauvinist aspirations he subscribed to in the 1930s in particular. The use of blubo terminology again here is, of course, extremely problematic given Heidegger's full-throated support for Nazism for a period of time. Nevertheless, the theoretical story we can tell concerning an authentic commu-nity living in accord with our essence as human beings is one that underwrites the need to acknowledge how other peoples, cultures, and communities are 'grounded' in similar ways. What is needed is a way of acknowledging and

---

[61] Though it must be said that relationality alone can seem rather flimsy and overly exsanguinated in its own right.

[62] See Mahon O'Brien (2015) for a detailed discussion of this.

preserving our specificity, our ability to be at home in time and place, to resist the dissolution of difference, without succumbing to the idea that inclusivity or cultural diversity are inherently problematic.

A View from Some-where (and When)

Seamus Heaney tirelessly excavated the way identity can be rooted and nourished in the rural and the agrarian. He frequently reflects on how he is both from and of the land of his childhood. However, he doesn't meditate only on the fields, hedges, meadows, trees, woods, rivers and streams of his childhood; he is rooted through time and place with and, in part, by 'people' as well.[63] The people in Heidegger's celebrated 'place', conversely, are very sparingly described. There is a severity, an austerity to his description of them, which is telling in its own way. The account of the irreducibly relational character of Dasein is rather anaemic in its own right when left undeveloped. That is not to say that Heidegger is debarred from doing so as a result of any theoretical necessity or inadequacy. However, when he has occasion to add some flesh to the bones of the people he lives among and with, we hear little of the intimacy of the ties of kinship, of family, of friendship.[64]

And yet, 'if self is a location', a self that finds itself in and of a time and place, what of 'love'?[65] What of the *people* who mark place? The ties of love,

---

[63] I am thinking here of the way one can feel haunted by the presence and memory of others. It's often people that are called to mind when we visit a place after a long absence. Indeed, it can often seem as though the hints and traces of some people trail around after us no matter where we go. Heaney captures the latter sentiment with characteristic heft in a poem called "Follower":

> All I ever did was follow
> In his broad shadow round the farm.
>
> I was a nuisance, tripping, falling,
> Yapping always. But today
> It is my father who keeps stumbling
> Behind me, and will not go away. (Heaney, 2018: 8)

[64] One could supplement this with some of Irigaray's compelling insights concerning Heidegger's failure to acknowledge sexuate difference in his account of Dasein. Irigaray returned to this problem in a recent volume containing long essays from four contributors. For a detailed discussion of my own views on this, see my contribution to that volume – "The Destitution of Dasein". (Irigaray, 2022).

[65] The relevant lines from Heaney's poem ("Aerodrome") are as follows:

> would she rise and go
> With the airman under his nose-up Thunderbolt
>
> Offering her a free seat in his cockpit?
> But for her part, in response, only the slightest
> Back-stiffening and standing of her ground
> As her hand reached down and tightened round my hand.

friendship, and community that bind are not exactly powerfully conveyed through depictions of dour, pipe-smoking cohorts, sporadically sharing clipped platitudes concerning the day's toil – joyless, and celebrated for their joylessness, their silence and severity, their austere economy of word, gesture, dare I say even, intimacy. For Heaney, the farmer is "hooped to where he planted (Heaney, 1988)", we find ourselves hooped to place – but does place hold for us in such profound ways simply because it is place? What makes it place? Do we only hear the 'silent call of the earth' and its seasons? Or is it a space and place we share with *others* – through ties of language, family, friendship, and indeed the tacit alliances formed through ties to place. Heidegger opens the door for these insights but does little in the end to furnish them or flesh them out.

Venturing out one autumn morning from the apartment I was renting in Lewes, a small town in the South Downs in the south east of England, not long after I began working at the University of Sussex and heading for the train to campus, my nose was filled with the unmistakable odour of a farmyard. The brisk air that rasped against my cheeks and swished through my nostrils with its sweet yet pungent fragrance immediately conjured up the image of my Grandfather, my father's father, a farmer from the South of Ireland, moving through the farmyard in the direction of the milking parlour and past a row of old stables and outhouses, while the waft of cattle, horses, the granary, silage, hay, and dung, all somehow magically distilled into one simultaneously heavy yet vibrant scent on the air, came back to me as well. I could see my grandfather ('the Bossman', as he was known by all and sundry) stooped slightly and shuffling along in front of me as a I made my way down the steep lane towards the train station. The smell alone had the capacity to transport, to reignite a sense of belonging and communion, with a family and an agricultural community in Ireland, of course, but also suddenly with people in this part of the world who work the land, who keep horses – people whom I only 'know' from the distant view of farmyards, walled meadows, and the busy smell of farming cutting through the chill morning air. The arc of this community widened to include not just people engaged in the husbandry of land stretching back at least a century in Ireland but also now in the south-east of England. Such is the potency of these experiences.

In other work I have pitched the insights and inclusivity of a number of Irish writers against some of Heidegger's most problematic texts from the 1930s in

---

If self is a location, so is love:
Bearings taken, markings, cardinal points,
Options, obstinacies, dug heels and distance,
Here and there and now and then, a stance. (Heaney, 2011)

particular.[66] Indeed, I would submit that these writers embrace a view that comes closer to the position that Heidegger underwrites in "Letter on Humanism", one that better fits the accounts of Dasein and death that he first ventures in *Being and Time* than some of his own more problematic work in the 1930s. Patrick Kavanagh, for instance, knew only too well the inner tensions of an identity forged in a rural village before relocating to pursue a literary life in the bustling city. Kavanagh nurtured his 'voice' while farming the land in a rural setting in Ulster until his poetic and literary ambitions brought him to Dublin. And yet, while he does not scruple to valorise and exalt his rural existence and what he learned there – his vision does not blind itself to what detracts from that same vision; his depictions, as always, are warts and all. True, he exalts certain experiences of his country life to the status of epiphanies at times, but he does not succumb to romantic excess; he concedes shortcomings (sometimes savagely) – for instance, the astonishing claim that his farming neighbours "cannot perceive Irony or even Satire". And yet, he protests in a poem called "Living in the Country":

> my intention is not satire but humaneness,
> An eagerness to understand more about sad man,
> Frightened man, the workers of the world,
> Without being savaged in the process.
> Broadness is my aim, a broad road where the many
> Can see life easier – generally. (Kavanagh, 2018: 48)

In "Epic" – a wonderful poetic distillation of the inner tensions he experienced – Kavanagh imagines Homer conjuring the *Iliad* from out of something akin to a local row that he witnessed between farmers in Ireland over a plot of land:

> That was the year of the Munich bother. Which
> Was more important? I inclined
> To lose my faith in Ballyrush and Gortin
> Till Homer's ghost came whispering to my mind.
> He said: I made the Iliad from such
> A local row. Gods make their own importance. (Kavanagh, 2018: 42)

Regardless of whether Kavanagh's poem is a genuine, earnest attempt to rehabilitate his fascination with the local (though I would argue that it is), even the surface meaning of the poem reinforces something vital to our argument. The local gravity through which we find ourselves grounded as human beings of a time and place is often the most immediate access we have to something like, in this instance, conflict. A quarrel between local farmers over

---

[66] See O'Brien (2015, 2025).

a plot of land in Monaghan shares something with the clash of nations for people in other parts of the world. That row was at the centre of affairs in Kavanagh's world at one time, his understanding of everything was tied to a place and time, and in this local conflict, there was access to conflict in a different place, on a wider scale. Otherwise, the 'Munich bother' would be remote and inaccessible. That is the point of the interjection from Homer's ghost.

Moreover, the use of the term 'Gods' here clearly echoes something we have been trying to unlock in Heidegger's account (see Heidegger's discussion of Heraclitus above) – the way the world worlds for an historical people will happen in ways specific to that people with their gods. Its meaning and importance emerge in *that* way for *that* people, with their godly narratives. What is more, that is the gateway to our recognition of the world worlding for other people in other times and places. Where Heidegger spends so much time exclusively trying to prospect and delve deeper 'within' the world he identifies with, these writers plumb familiar depths in search of other frequencies and currents, passageways to other worlds, and then explore both the continuity and the productive tensions between them, that is, between the local, national, and international.[67] One can simultaneously be nourished and claimed by all of them in different yet interweaving ways. We can exist as intelligible palimpsests, multi-layered 'texts', bearing the cultural and historical marks and traces of a unique identity.

Perhaps the advantage of both Heaney and Kavanagh over Heidegger here is that they have experienced the dual sense of exile and belonging such that they are less inclined to artificially foreclose the avenues of recognition and understanding. Kavanagh saw himself as an inner émigré in the hectic urban life of Dublin and describes the epiphanies that he continually experienced while immersed in a rural, agricultural life in Monaghan. Nonetheless, he still managed to connect these epiphanies to frequencies and traditions that pulled him out of that familiar landscape. Indeed, he celebrates his ability to grow "with nature again as before" (Kavanagh. 2018: 50) along a city canal bank – memorialised forever now in a famous poem ("Canal Bank Walk").

The fanaticism that characterised Heidegger's attempts to mobilise some of his philosophical views in the service of his politics betokened, to some extent perhaps, the urgency of his own place and time. Even so, while calling for revolution, he oversteps the bounds of his own thought. There is, as a consequence, a lack of the conciliatory, a rigidity in outlook and disposition,

---

[67] On one occasion, Heaney expresses his delight at the opportunity to discuss his work at a small celebration in his local community following the award of the Nobel Prize for literature. He describes it as "a kind of confirmation on the home ground of what was said from the outside". (see www.youtube.com/watch?v=HxqEK1nUeA4 Accessed 16 April 2024).

which looks to exclude and include in the same stroke. Heidegger allows his thinking, in a way, to be radicalised or to posture as though it should be. He looks to disqualify all 'city-folk', for example, from having any business in coming to the countryside:

> The world of the city runs the risk of falling into a destructive error. A very loud and very active and very fashionable obtrusiveness often passes itself off as concern for the world and existence of the peasant. But this goes exactly contrary to the one and only thing that now needs to be done, namely, to keep one's distance from the life of the peasant, to leave their existence more than ever to its own law, to keep hands off lest it be dragged into the literati's dishonest chatter about 'folk-character' and 'rootedness in the soil' ... nowadays many people from the city ... often behave in the village or at a farmer's house in the same way they 'have fun' at their recreation centers in the city. Such goings-on destroy more in one evening than centuries of scholarly teaching about folk-character and folklore could ever hope to promote. (GA13: 12/29)[68]

In a letter to his wife, dating from his time on active military duty, the depth of Heidegger's enmity to urban life is unmistakable – a sectarianism of sorts which is most disquieting:

> Yesterday evening we did something special, travelled to Berlin & had a look at the bustle on Friedrichstrasse ... both of us [were] **disgusted to the marrow** ... now I do understand Berlin better ... it lacks what is simply Great and Divine. When I think of Freibg. [Freiburg] & its Minster & the outlines of the Black Forest mountains ... The people here have lost their soul ... perhaps the 'spirit' of Berlin can be overcome by a home-grown culture at the provincial universities – at any rate our youth will only be restored to health from this quarter – if it's possible at all. (Heidegger, 2008: 45 Emphasis added)

Heinrich Petzet, in a perverse and self-defeating attempt to paint a sympathetic picture and convey the sensitivity of Heidegger, confirms Heidegger's enduring aversion to urban life:

> Heidegger was slightly suspicious of everything that had to do with the city and never quite felt comfortable in it ... **In simply getting close to a big city** – with its proliferating dump sites, factories, and desolate housing developments, with the whole ugly atmosphere of formless and rampant growth that surrounds even old and beautiful cities – **Heidegger, an extremely sensitive man, would be affected with almost physical abhorrence** ... If Heidegger lacked a certain 'ubranity' and was estranged from everything pertaining to city life, this was particularly so in the case of the urbane spirit of the Jewish circles in the large cities of the West. (Petzet, 1993: 33–34 Emphasis added)

---

[68] Translation taken from Sheehan (2010).

What are we to make of this rustic provincialism (not to mention the antisemitism which I have discussed at length elsewhere)?[69] It is in many ways indefensible – that much is presumably obvious from our analysis. But how does this fit with our attempts to discover an originary ethics in Heidegger? What if we were to strip away or excise the ethnic chauvinism and the exclusionary aspects of Heidegger's vision, laced as it is with so much animus to city life? I warrant that, for many of us, the fact that our capacity to understand is shaped by the people and places that we take our bearings from is not in itself something we would recoil from. That *is* often how we find our bearings, after all; and we navigate accordingly. We do not have to embrace Heidegger's insistence on a radical discontinuity between the bearings of a mud-larking city-dweller and a country ruffian gambolling through the meadows. In other words, we (human beings) face a temporal horizon which orients all of us in similar ways, ways that converge and intersect as much as they divide and distinguish, so long as we look for commonality and do not treat as alien those who, despite other differences, bleed, die, love, laugh, and find themselves 'thrown' very much as we do. Why should verisimilitude be exclusively a quality of rural life when that type of existence will be touched by technology every bit as much as the city? *Gestell* is not the preserve of the city, and it is naïve (and needlessly divisive) to suppose that the appropriate response is to build an invisible wall around rural communities to protect them from the ravages of urbanisation and the toxic influence of cosmopolitan aliens. In his monocular focus on rural life in Southern Germany, Heidegger at once appears to see it as a haven from the deleterious influence of *Gestell* while acknowledging already that the countryside is feeling its effects. The dangers of the technological age are ones that we collectively face – the effects are felt everywhere and by everyone. As John Healy observes in his memoirs, reflecting on the changes that swept through the landscape of his childhood in the West of Ireland:

> Above in Dublin now we are already worrying about the cultural impact of electronic technology and the effect which television, with its Anglo-American values, was having on rural Ireland. We talked about it as if it was the first wave of technology and the only one which would have a fearsome cultural spin-off. [On] this part of the hill it was an academic argument: many of the houses were empty and all the waves of ad-massery could sweep over this hillside and it didn't matter. Another, and earlier, technology had already altered the cultural patterns and we had never recognized it or seen what it was doing to our people. (Healy, 1987: 119)

---

[69] See O'Brien (2015, 2022).

Adorno ridicules what he sees as the pretentious solemnity of Heidegger's attempts to characterise his own work as directly comparable to that of the peasant farmers he so admires.[70] And yet, we find echoes of these sentiments expressed in ways that don't appear to be quite so farcical or unctuous in Heaney:

> The cold smell of potato mould, the squelch and slap
> Of soggy peat, the curt cuts of an edge
> Through living roots awaken in my head.
> But I've no spade to follow men like them.
> Between my finger and my thumb
> The squat pen rests.
> I'll dig with it. (Heaney, 2018: 4)

The issue is ultimately one of exclusion versus inclusion. The writers I have mentioned here appear to see the local as a gateway to a *wider world*. Heidegger explicitly looked to block any form of universalism as though it were tainted with the metaphysics of presence. In this, he appears at times to have suppressed some of the implications of his own thought. To avoid confusion, perhaps, we should try to limit our use of terms like 'universal' or 'cosmopolitan', since they clearly carry the baggage of anonymity and a metaphysics that Heidegger is allergic to. To poach (and repurpose) a phrase from Gregory Fried, we could say that we are dealing with a "situated transcendence", and a productive strife between the local and the 'foreign'.[71] Either way, and more importantly, we must avoid the tendency to valorise or privilege one kind of groundedness in place and time, in tradition, as though it were superior or 'more authentic' to another. We should instead look for ways to facilitate recognition and inclusion, as opposed to exclusion, prejudice, ethnic chauvinism, what have you. To not recognise 'others' in these ways is to fail in our ethical obligations to them, to dehumanise them, to not see them as 'outstanding' beings with their own gravities of time and place. Indeed, it is this failure to see other human beings as 'mortals' that Heidegger, as we saw in Section 2, condemns as an ethical failing in some of his remarks in Bremen.[72]

Conclusion

Both Plato and Aristotle, at least on my reading, recognise that we cannot treat the 'science of human affairs' as an exact science. Philosophical inquiries into

---

[70] See Adorno (2003: 43–45).

[71] See Fried (2021). Fried does a wonderful job unpacking some of the relevant arguments in Heidegger. Ultimately, he finds in favour of Plato over Heidegger when it comes to the question of our ability to formulate a viable ethics. Fried's argument relies on a critique of relativism that he applies to Heidegger, one that we have challenged in the foregoing.

[72] Of course, the challenge again is to see how we can undertake this kind of thinking and discourse without resorting to absolute, timeless principles.

ethics or morality need to proceed differently. Their inquiries into the good life, virtue, and justice, for instance, possess a theoretical humility, and therefore a sophistication and nuance, that makes them very much relevant today. Heidegger, for his part, seems to have hit on something that many of us readily recognise in terms of our radical contingency, our finitude, our thrown situatedness, and the fact that we 'find' ourselves as members of historical communities with traditions and commitments, along with, as an inevitable consequence, a relative perspective or outlook on things. However, as Vogel argues, approaching ethics in this way runs the risk of simply reproducing the problems we face with the existentialist reading of Heidegger, where now, instead of dealing with the identity of the individual subject and its radical subjectivity, we have the same kind of identity writ large as an historical community, which may well issue in provincialism, exclusion, and/or ethnic chauvinism.[73] The challenge then is to identify something 'general', something that binds us, but without suppressing or ignoring how our commitments are 'locally' situated and motivated.

The most we might be able to canvass for is a recognition that we 'are' as people only insofar as we are shaped by the finitude and history that shapes any and every human community. Moreover, it is also clear that not every culture will mark birth, death, and the various milestones that chart the course of our lives in the same ways. Indeed, we may not even integrate as individuals into our society in the same ways. Customs and mores, laws and norms will differ, at times markedly. Nevertheless, in the same way that we are encouraged to see other people as being-towards-death, we can resist Heidegger's perverse attempt in the 1930s to isolate an historical community in self-sustaining non-relationality before it ventures forth to be with other communities afterwards. We are always already 'with' other communities and other 'peoples' – the notion of a 'pure' society living in splendid isolation is, quite simply, a fantasy, and an inhuman one at that.

Thus, we can begin to think of our ethical obligations to others, in keeping with Heidegger's account, without falling foul of some of the problems that blight his own attempts for a time to appropriate his own thinking in infelicitous ways. We can say that we are the beings that are called to and bound by time and place, to place as a site for the emergence of our history and our language as the eventuation of word. In other words, that which distinguishes us is simultaneously what unites us. In the same way that I feel a call of sorts and am aware of my past, my family, loved ones, friends, home, everything that gives meaning and depth to my life, that leaves me feeling forlorn or nostalgic at times and wanting to hold on to certain experiences – to savour and cherish them, I can see

---

[73] Indeed, Heidegger himself charged at full tilt in those directions during the 1930s.

other people in other places as having meaning and depth in their lives in similar ways. This very recognition might well be the key to grounding an ethics. We can further say that to acknowledge that norms are relative is not to deny that we are commonly enjoined as ethical beings – that we are bound ethically in the same basic ways. This in turn can serve as the basis for dialogue and mediation when our norms and values conflict; it allows us to identify our shared essence as human beings, that is, as ethical beings.

Recently, in the dwindling light and quiet melancholy of an early January evening, I wandered around the garden paths of my childhood home; smoke from a wood fire lingered on the still air, as it has done so many times before. I was mulling over some of the questions posed in this book while awaiting news of my sister who had gone into labour that morning. In the midst of my rambles, it occurred to me that I often think of others as being hooped and placed (i.e., as people) in similar ways to the way I feel at home in this place – surrounded by my family. I am often moved by this observation when I see someone whose life has taken a turn for the worse, or someone who perhaps is on the other side of a dispute that I myself am invested in, people I can look on as alien to me in some way or, in the latter case, as not deserving of my concern or beneficence. In those moments I often imagine that person innocently playing with their friends as a child, oblivious to the challenges life invariably levies us with – surrounded by the love and security offered by parents, family, and home – cocooned and safe within the environs of the familiar.[74] And, in those very moments, I find my sense of enmity or distance diminishes and my sympathy swells. On this particular evening, I found myself thinking of all of the people I might see myself as distanced from in some way as at one time being waited on anxiously by parents, family, friends – just as we now anxiously awaited news of my niece's impending birth. I thought of how this placed history of ours was about to be shared with a new historical Dasein. Later, along with the news of her safe arrival, came the announcement of my niece's name – 'Lily Úna'.[75] The name 'Lily Úna' would now blossom as a name of this place and our time, becoming a part of the meaning and history of this home and these pathways – a name to be woven into the fragile fabric of our time and place, the tissued tiers of our time together, sharing in the fragility and marked by the way that meaningfulness is set against the nameless, another name, another calling (*heißen* in German has the double sense of name and call) that 'stands out' into the nameless. Lily of *our* valley – on the earth, under the sky,

---

[74] In the case of people whom I know to have been less fortunate than that, I find myself feeling enormous pity that they did not enjoy the comfort and security of my own childhood.

[75] Úna is my mother's name. It is an Irish name whose origin is, from what I can ascertain, unclear. However, it is possibly derived from the Irish word for 'lamb' (*úan*).

one of 'us', facing into the nothingness against which our world is set – in Muingboy, with its winding garden paths, and the hip-roofed house that shelters us against wind, rain, and cold, that opens up to receive the sunshine and warm breezes in the Summer. This is the home where we break bread together, drink wine, toast births and triumphs, mourn the loss of loved ones, and mark the milestones of their lives with us. Together, we watch the garden wither and withdraw against the cold in winter only to blossom forth again in the rain and sun of spring. We sleep and wake together in this house as a growing family, each of us bound to the place and playing a part in the history of our home. The unity of the fourfold issues forth in the appearance to us of our home *as* our home. Other people from other times and places must similarly feel "wordless joy at having once more withstood want, trembling before the impending birth, and shivering at the surrounding menace of death" (GA5: 19/*Off the Beaten Track*, 14). I think of others in this way, and I cannot help but think of being bound ethically by this thought.

Of course, that does not tell us what to do in a specific situation or even necessarily what is right or wrong, but it prevents the exclusionary, alienating move that is cited as a problem for Heidegger's account of both authentic Dasein and the authentic Dasein of a people. If everyone is recognised and acknowledged as being human in these ways, then, as argued earlier, we cannot leverage nearly as much from our differences as people might suppose. We cannot dehumanise people whose essence is grounded by the gravity of their own time and place, as though they are radically different from ourselves, when that is how we derive meaning, significance, and obligation in our own lives.

Conversely, insisting on abstract, universal principles in the hope of eradicating any trace or possibility of prejudice ignores an uncomfortable fact: our moral intuitions, our allegiances, our motives for acting in certain situations, are frequently tied to a sense of familiarity, community, regionality. We introduce checks and balances to try and maintain fairness insofar as we can. But we must not demand too much of ourselves. We cannot pretend that we are going to be as motivated to help a stranger in East Bengal as we might be to help or safeguard our own children, spouses, or loved ones. To insist on devising principles that demand that we do as much is a sort of ascetic ideal that reminds us of the austere economy of desire and mortification of the flesh we associate with the very worst elements of Catholicism.

Recognising that we are not born pre-programmed to adopt Kant's reasoning is not to abandon ourselves to 'evaluative nihilism'. It is this unwitting commitment to either theism or Kantianism (or their opposite) which has led readers of Nietzsche and Heidegger astray again and again. To think ethically requires us to see clearly the essence of the human being. As individuals and as communities, a certain transparency as to how we have been shaped by forbearers who signified and marked our placed history allows us to self-consciously accept, repeat, cherish, adapt, and indeed modify the rituals, practices, and beliefs of that community. We can feel ties of kinship and community, but that does not necessitate that our historical borders be rigid; our cultural cartography can still be a constant work in progress. Our history has been and will continue to be marked by insights and conversations generated within and without. In the same way that our language bears the traces and marks of different traditions, so do our historical communities and traditions continue to evolve and interweave. And, in seeing how we come from places and times, how we belong to historical communities, we can see how other communities are expressive of that peoples' placed time as they revolve around the same kind of temporal and regional magnetic poles that orient all of us. We may not feel compelled by the obligations, customs, or mores of our neighbours (situated as they are in the place of their own time), but we can at least recognise the basis for their commitments. Recognising other human beings as 'out-standing' beings, those beings who 'stand out' into the nothing, facing the namelessness that silently announces itself in their named situatedness, is key to establishing our ethical bond. It may not immediately issue in solutions to specific moral dilemmas or conflicts, but it can certainly serve as the basis for opening a dialogue and looking for common ground, resolution, reconciliation. Some might be tempted to go further and look to formulate imperatives that can issue in concrete rules or injunctions. However, it might prove more prudent to accept that we live in a world where human beings will be motivated to pursue the interests of themselves and those closest to them before all else, a world where there is an incommensurability of desires and thus the inevitability of conflict. If we want to make that world safe for ourselves and others, we need to promote dialogue and avoid absolutism and fanaticism. People need to recognise, therefore, that those with whom we would contend in the trials and contests of life are, at the very least, even if they belong to different cultures and traditions, 'mortals' very much as we are. Even as we petition for our own needs over theirs (which should not perhaps be censured with the frosty, faux piety of the absolutist), we may find that our demands will be tempered by that very recognition.

I believe that Heidegger would argue that, by and large, people are not motivated by abstract principles; they are motivated by what matters to them. The human 'project' may be endlessly littered with failures, but perhaps it is time to relinquish the procrustean desire for absolute timeless rules when what we are faced with is an enormous project of mediation and communication. Granted, we may not be able to prove that unspeakable atrocities are wrong owing to their failure to survive something like a deontological calculation.

Nevertheless, the delusional scrupulousness (however well-intentioned) of such approaches cannot alter or account for the joint facts of relativism and ethical dissensus the world over. Maybe this is down to the fact that such approaches have not successfully identified and thought through the real source and motivation of our ethical obligations. Perhaps the people who are already radicalised in such a way as to think that their imperatives and compulsions are timeless and categorical are the very ones who need to recognise at least how their beliefs may be better understood as having a different origin. That in itself might foster a willingness to at least listen to diverging views. Perhaps the appropriate response to the charge of evaluative nihilism, or relativism, is to acknowledge that variance and perspectivalism owing to historical situatedness are unavoidable – but that that is *not* to resign ourselves to nihilism. We do not have to accept this false dichotomy – that is, *either* absolute moral imperatives *or* amoral nihilism.[76] Values, customs, traditions, and beliefs *have been and continue to be* relative from one historical period and community to another. Rather than toiling in vain in the service of absolutist fantasies, why not focus our energies instead on fostering dialogue and recognition? Why not try to demonstrate that what we *all* cherish within our specific lives and communities stems from our thrown, finite situatedness – as mortals, on the earth, underneath the sky, facing into the abyss, and cleaving to the worlds and places we feel at home in? Heidegger's contribution to ethics might seem elliptical to some in that he does not furnish us with much more than this. Nevertheless, he clearly believes that understanding properly for the first time our essence as human beings will itself be transformative.

I will leave the final words to an Irish poet whom I have invoked a number of times in previous sections, Seamus Heaney. In a 1989 interview, Heaney is pressed on his heritage, his political views, his identity as an Irish Catholic from the North of Ireland, and his apparent retreat from a more unequivocal, politically charged Nationalism that the interviewer attributes to some earlier poems. Heaney's words are ablutionary and edifying – humanism and humaneness at their very best. The poet knows only too well that "within the very watermark of their [Catholics and Protestants in the North of Ireland] psyche there's a sniff of the division", a sniff of "a living rift".[77] Nevertheless, he is steadfast in his commitment to the power of language to communicate and mediate, to recognise, even in communities heavily marked by division. Co-existence amid subtle (if unmistakable) and not-so-subtle divisions has been, and can again be, possible:

---

[76] Hatab offers a similar observation. (See Hatab, 2000: 88)

[77] Interview with Seamus Heaney. "All This is Part of Me" (1974). www.rte.ie/archives/exhib itions/1982-seamus-heaney/1989-northern-ireland-troubles/606394-literary-conscription/.

Heaney: I suppose I've been over-sensitive, maybe, of saying things that would make them [Protestant community] feel that they weren't utterly welcome … under the cultural umbrella of an Irish nation …This is a very complicated territory. They [Protestant community] perceive I suppose, the provisional campaign as a racist campaign. And I perceive the Provisionals as taking over certain ground that everybody has a right to, you know, so you can get accused of being slyly green and at the same time therefore … failing the Protestants and failing to stand up enough for the utter greenness …

Hanly: Well, how do you answer that? …

Heaney: I don't think I have to answer that!

Hanly: You don't?

Heaney: The thing is that people set terms that are too simple … I have had, from the moment I began to breathe, an instinctive sense of the velleities and dangers and the underground life of … Protestant/Catholic [in the North of Ireland]. I think it's extremely subtle; I think that language that is used to talk about it is like sledgehammers usually; whereas the reality changes by faint milli-tilts. One of the most important things and moving things that happened to me in my life was when I got a degree from Queen's [Queen's University Belfast] six years ago, an honorary degree; the Vice Chancellor of the university talked about this … ex-student [Heaney], in terms of being from *his country*; he didn't say Ulster or the province … [this was] somebody prominent in Northern establishment, Unionist circles conceding by a discreet diction a dimension of Irishness; **now, to me, those graces and subtleties are the tilt of the world … it isn't the gallow that moves it … and therefore I would like to negotiate at that level**. (Emphasis added)[78]

---

[78] Interview with Seamus Heaney (1989) www.rte.ie/archives/exhibitions/1982-seamus-heaney/1989-northern-ireland-troubles/606417-dealing-with-northern-ireland/. Accessed 17 April 2024.

Bibliography

Adorno, Theodor. *The Jargon of Authenticity*. Translated by Knut Tarnowski and Frederic Will. London and New York: Routledge, 2003.

Bergo, Bettina. "'Sterben Sie?': The Problem of Dasein and 'Animals' . . . of Various Kinds". In *Heidegger's Black Notebooks: Responses to Anti-Semitism*. Edited by Andrew J. Mitchell and Peter Trawny. New York: Columbia University Press, 2017, pp. 52–73.

Caputo, John D. *Radical Hermeneutics : Repetition, Deconstruction, and the Hermeneutic Project*. Bloomington and Indianapolis: Indiana University Press, 1987.

Dahlstrom, Daniel. *The Heidegger Dictionary* (2nd ed.). London: Bloomsbury, 2023.

Di Cesare, Donatella. "The 'Jewish Question' and the Question of Being: Heidegger before and after 1945". *Journal of Aesthetics and Phenomenology*, 4:2(2017), 173–182.

Edwards, James C. "The Thinging of the Thing: The Ethic of Conditionality in Heidegger's Later Work". In *A Companion to Heidegger*. Edited by Hubert L. Dreyfus and Mark A. Wrathall. Oxford: Blackwell, 2005, pp. 456–467.

Ellmann, Richard. *James Joyce*. Oxford: Oxford University Press, 1982.

Faye, Emmanuel. "Being, History, Technology, and Extermination in the Work of Heidegger". *Journal of the History of Philosophy*, 50:1(January 2012), 111–130.

Freeman, Lauren. "Metontology, Moral Particularism, and the 'Art of Existing': A Dialogue between Heidegger, Aristotle, and Bernard Williams". *Continental Philosophy Review*. 43(2010), 545–568.

Fried, Gregory. *Towards a Polemical Ethics: Between Heidegger and Plato*. Lanham: Rowman & Littlefield, 2021.

Golob, Sacha. "Heidegger's Ethics". In *The Cambridge History of Moral Philosophy*. Edited by Sacha Golob and Jens Timmerman. Cambridge: Cambridge University Press, 2017, pp. 623–635.

Hatab, Lawrence. *Ethics and Finitude: Heideggerian Contributions to Moral Philosophy*. Lanham: Rowman & Littlefield, 2000.

Healy, John. *Nineteen Acres*. Achill: House of Healy, 1987.

Heaney, Seamus. *District and Circle*. London: Faber & Faber, 2011.

New Selected Poems: 1966–1987. London: Faber & Faber, 1988.

100 Poems. London: Faber & Faber, 2018.

Heidegger, Martin. *Sein und Zeit. Tübingen: Niemeyer, 1967*. English Translation: *Being and Time*. Translated by John Macquarrie & Edward Robinson. Oxford: Blackwell, 1962.

Aus der Erfahrung des Denkens. Gesamtausgabe, Volume 13. Edited by Hermann Heidegger. Frankfurt am Main: Klostermann, 1983. English Translation of "'Schöpferische Landschaft: Warum Bleiben wir in der Provinz?': 'Why do I Stay in the Provinces?'". Translated by Thomas Sheehan. In *Heidegger: the Man and the Thinker*. Edited by Thomas Sheehan. New Brunswick: Transaction Publishers, 2010.

Bremer und Freiburger Vortraege. Gesamtausgabe, Volume 79. Edited by Petra Jaeger. Frankfurt am Main: Klostermann, 1994. English Translation: *Bremen and Freiburg Lectures: Insight Into That Which Is and Basic Principles of Thinking*. Translated by Andrew J. Mitchell. Bloomington and Indianapolis: Indiana University Press, 2012.

Die Grundbegriffe der Metaphysik: Welt – Endlichkeit – Einsamkeit. Gesamtausgabe, Volume 29/30. Edited by Friedrich-Wilhelm von Herrmann. Frankfurt am Main: Klostermann, 2004. English Translation: *The Fundamental Concepts of Metaphysics*: *World, Finitude, Solitude*. Translated by William McNeill and Nicholas Walker. Bloomington: Indiana University Press, 1995.

Einführung in die Metaphysik. Gesamtausgabe, Volume 40. Edited by Petra Jaeger. Frankfurt am Main: Klostermann, 1983. English Translation: *Introduction to Metaphysics*. Translated by Gregory Fried and Richard Polt. New Haven and London: Yale University Press, 2000.

Gelassenheit: Heideggers Meßkircher Rede von 1955. Freiburg/ München: Verlag Karl Alber, 2. Auflage), 2015.

Holzwege. Gesamtausgabe, Volume 5. Edited by Friedrich-Wilhelm Von Herrmann. Frankfurt am Main: Klostermann, 1950. English Translation: *Off the Beaten Track*. Edited and Translated by Julian Young and Kenneth Haynes. Cambridge: Cambridge University Press, 2002. Some Essays from *Holzwege* also Appear in *Basic Writings*. Edited by David Farrell Krell. New York : Harper & Row, 2008.

The Heidegger-Jaspers Correspondence (1920–1963). Edited by Walter Biemel and Hans Saner. Translated by Gary E. Aylesworth. Humanity Books, New York, 2003.

Wegmarken. Gesamtausgabe, Volume 9. Edited by Friedrich-Wilhelm von Herrmann. Frankfurt am Main: Klostermann, 1976. English translation: *Pathmarks*. Edited by William McNeill. Cambridge: Cambridge University Press, 1998.

Heidegger, Martin : *Vorträge und Aufsätze* (1936–1953). Edited by Friedrich-Wilhelm von Herrmann. Gesamtausgabe, Volume 7. Frankfurt am Main: Klostermann, 2000.

Letters to his Wife: 1915–1970. Selected, edited and annotated by Gertrud Heidegger. Translated by R. D. V. Glasgow. Cambridge: Polity Press, 2008.

Zollikoner Seminare, Protokolle-Gespraeche-Briefe. Edited by Medard Boss. Frankfurt am Main: Klostermann, 1987. English Translation: *Zollikon Seminars: Protocols-Conversations-Letters.* Edited by Medard Boss. Translated by Franz Mayr and Richard Askay. Evanston: Northwestern University Press, 2001.

Hodge, Joanna. *Heidegger and Ethics.* London: Routledge, 1995.

Kavanagh, Patrick. *The Great Hunger.* London: Penguin, 2018.

McMullin, Irene. *Time and the Shared World: Heidegger on Social Relations.* Evanston: Northwestern University Press, 2013.

McNeill, William. *The Fate of Phenomenology: Heidegger's Legacy.* Lanham: Rowman & Littlefield, 2020.

Mitchell, Andrew J. *The Fourfold: Reading the Late Heidegger.* Evanston: Northwestern University Press, 2015.

Speeches that Changed the World. With an Introduction by Simon Sebag Montefiore. London: Quercus, 2006.

Nancy, Jean-Luc. "Heidegger's 'Originary Ethics'". In *Heidegger and Practical Philosophy.* Edited by François Raffoul and David Pettigrew. Albany: State University of New York Press, 2002.

Nietzsche, Friedrich. *The Gay Science.* Edited by Walter Kaufmann. New York: Vintage, 1974.

O'Brien, Mahon. "Contra Heidegger: The 'Local', 'National', and 'International' in Joyce, Kavanagh, and Heaney". In *Irish Phenomenology: A Continental Philosophy of Ireland.* Edited by Daniel Bradley and Roisin Lally. London and New York: Rowman & Littlefield, 2025.

"Death, Politics, and Heidegger's Bremen Remarks". *The Southern Journal of Philosophy*, 60:2(2022), 249–276.

Heidegger and Authenticity: From Resoluteness to Releasement. New York and London: Bloomsbury, 2013.

Heidegger, History and the Holocaust. New York and London: Bloomsbury, 2015.

Heidegger's Life and Thought: A Tarnished Legacy. London: Rowman & Littlefield, 2020.

"Irigaray and Plato – Unlikely Bedfellows". *Journal of the British Society for Phenomenology*, 52:2(2021): Phenomenology and Ancient Greek Philosophy.

"The Destitution of Dasein". *In Challenging a Fictitious Neutrality: Heidegger in Question*. Edited by Luce Irigaray. Palgrave Macmillan, 2022, pp. 13–72.

O'Brien, Pat. *A History of Broadford Parish, Co. Clare: The Civil Parishes of Kilseily and Killokennedy 1800–1850*. Limerick: The Celtic Bookshop, 2022.

Olafson, Frederick A. *Heidegger and the Ground of Ethics: A Study of Mitsein*. Cambridge: Cambridge University Press, 1998.

The Compact Edition of the Oxford English Dictionary. Oxford: Oxford University Press, 1979.

Petzet, Heinrich. *Encounters and Dialogues with Martin Heidegger 1929–1976*. Translated by Parvis Emad and Kenneth Maly. Chicago: The University of Chicago Press, 1993.

Heidegger: The Man and the Thinker. Edited by Thomas Sheehan. New Brunswick: Transaction Publishers, 2010.

The Heidegger Controversy: A Critical Reader. Edited by Richard Wolin. Cambridge, MA: The MIT Press, 1993.

Safranski, Rudiger. *Martin Heidegger: Between Good and Evil*. Translated by Ewald Osers. Cambridge, MA: Harvard University Press, 1998.

Thomson, Iain. "Rethinking Levinas on Heidegger on Death". *The Harvard Review of Philosophy*. XVI(Fall 2009).

Vogel, Lawrence. *The Fragile "We" Ethical Implications of Heidegger's "Being and Time"*. Evanston: Northwestern University Press, 1994.

Williams, Bernard. "Human Prejudice". The Walter E. Edge Lecture, Princeton University, 15 October 2002. www.youtube.com/watch?v=SqQ4Dv_0984 (Accessed 06/12/2023).

To Ana and Daisy

who have widened the arc of my sense of home